The
GOD
Dilemma

Nathan Driscoll

malcolm down

PUBLISHING

24 23 22 21 20 7 6 5 4 3 2 1

First published 2020 by Malcolm Down Publishing Ltd.
www.malcolmdown.co.uk

British Library Cataloguing in Publication Data
A catalogue record for this book is available from the British Library.

ISBN 978-1-912863-36-5

Cover design by Esther Kotecha

Art direction by Sarah Grace

Printed in the UK

Contents

Acknowledgements 5

Preface 7

Abstract 9

Introduction 13

Chapter 1: What Do We Know? 19

Chapter 2: The Mind-Body Debate 37

Chapter 3: Our Capacity for Intelligent Redesign...............49

Chapter 4: Rationality – Our Best Hope?............................67

Chapter 5: 'Rationality' – How does it apply to Evolution,
              Intentionality and Creationist Theology? 85

Chapter 6: Evolution as a Metatheory – a Reassessment 99

Chapter 7: Immanence and Evolution – are they compatible?..... 109

Chapter 8: Faith – a Catalyst for Oppression? 129

Chapter 9: The New Enlightenment Project 151

Chapter 10: Conclusion (1) – Spaces for Faith in Science 171

Chapter 11: Conclusion (2) – Human Nature –
              Can We Go It Alone? 187

Postscript 201

References... 203

Appendix 1 215

Appendix 2 223

Appendix 3 231

Index 237

Acknowledgements

I want to thank my wife, Jenny, who read through many of the chapters initially and has supported me throughout my endeavour to examine the philosophy behind atheism, agnosticism and belief. It's not really usual to go beyond this point in acknowledgements but as I am unlikely to have this opportunity again, I am going to break that rule. My wife is kind, humble and often self-effacing; she has a compassion which goes beyond my furthest expectations and I have the highest respect and deep love for her. I am much more than fortunate to have found her for my soulmate in my life.

The second person I want to thank is my friend Tim Edwards. He is a poet and a writer and has painstakingly gone through each page correcting my mediocre grammar and gently making suggestions. He is a more critical and sceptical friend, gently showing me where there have been flaws in my arguments and where a different point of view could also be taken. At the end of the first concluding chapter I reproduce a poem which he has written reflecting some of the relevant themes. I have included some of his comments in the second of the concluding chapters. He has given me his expertise without ever holding back and without him my thinking would be expressed in a far more hesitant way. He has added substance to the content. I am more than grateful to him. I should also thank my friend Bill Henderson for advising me not to start with what is now Chapter 7.

I also want to thank my friends The Very Venerable Gordon Kuhrt and Jeremy Firth for their immense enthusiasm and support while reading through some very dense and not always clear writing.

When I wrote this, I did not know if a publisher would be interested or not. I write under a pseudonym for professional reasons. I want to thank Malcolm Down for his encouragement and support and for giving me a chance to reach a wider audience. I would also like to thank his editor Chloe Evans for the painstaking work she has carried out to help me keep to the point, improve the presentation and develop the flow of the argument. I also want to thank our friend Elizabeth Wiggans for her invaluable and generous help in completing the index.

Finally, my daughters Eva and Sarah and their children, Thomas, Harry, Daniel, Sienna and Olivia: this is for them – I am not sure they will all ever read it but as the piece began to develop I decided that my target audience should be my grandchildren. This book is written in the hope that they will all lead fulfilling and purposeful lives – I hope they will realise that what sort of person you are is as important, if not more so, than what you do.

Preface

Recent study into the smallest particles and invisible forcefields in our universe are increasingly revealing the limits that the very process of scientific enquiry places on those findings. Against this, the intelligibility which has enabled us to discover the haphazard and random aspects of evolution is now being used to engineer our own genetic makeup and that of other species. Whatever we may think about the idea of a Creator God, there is no question that we, Homo sapiens, are redesigning nature. This has been brought about by our own capacity to cooperate and collaborate as well as through our burgeoning knowledge of the natural world.

We may have underrated the importance of meaning in comparison to the traditional methodologies of the natural sciences. Where do the empirical aspects of the world we have uncovered and the meaning we find within relationships meet? In other words, where do logic and feeling intersect? This debate has been running from time immemorial but as scientific knowledge has accelerated in the modern era the perceived distance between these polarities also continues to grow. One place they do meet is within ourselves, but just because they meet in 'us', they are not 'identical twins'. The methods we use to explore each of them are different, but they are both something we 'know'. We are talking about different types of 'knowing'.

How far can our rational powers take us? Have we the self-control to use our ever-increasing intelligence responsibly? Is there a place for humility in all of this? Many writers have long since discarded the notion of faith being a rational option, but as we find out more and more about what we do not know, this could very well be a premature conclusion. This book attempts to explore the spaces which science, rationality and faith occupy and poses the question as to whether or not they can coexist.

Abstract

Knowledge

Interpersonal knowledge is as relevant a form of knowledge as the traditional subject matter of physics, chemistry, biology and mathematics. The latter is often thought to be independent from what we call 'relationship' but there are significant contexts where this is not the case. For example, artificial selection means we can now 'select' for our own survival. This means that (a) we are no longer bound by Darwinian evolution, and (b) the creative, personal and social dimensions of human flourishing are all involved in 'selecting' for our own survival. Furthermore, the mind-body debate is no longer about a strict divide between the physical and the cognitive: physical systems can potentially incorporate genuine freedom of choice within the human brain, even if we are still in the process of discovering those systems.

Rationality

'Selecting' for our own survival involves the use of 'rationality'. In the context of human relationships and understanding, there is always more than one 'rational' outcome, as there are uses of the word 'rational' itself. 'Rationality' can take many different forms, one of which is the notion of being 'detached' and 'objective', namely, being able to structure thinking which is not simply confined to the thinker's environment. Another contrasting use is the idea of acting for the 'wellbeing' of others. I maintain that one core element of 'rationality', however it is defined, is a structure of internal coherence into which various semantic notions of the concept can be integrated. Practical rationality is not removed from human influences – it is part and parcel of it. Reasoning is an invaluable tool in determining social policy, but human beings are a mixture of feelings, physical dispositions and cognitive creativity: reason cannot fully control all those factors, including the impulsive and buried histories in everyone's life. Rationality which relies on reason for practical applications is a necessary, if not sufficient 'compass' for the betterment of human society.

Evolution

The debate over the significance of evolution involves the denunciation of religion as a mythological smokescreen and, worse still, justification for abuse which is fuelled by a judgemental religious ideology. My argument is that evolution is not the 'theory to end all theories' it is sometimes advertised as, that is, within the context of science. The accusation that religion is often misused is well founded, but the removal of religion does not reveal an innocence in human nature: human nature is fallible with or without religion, and this is compatible with the 'survival of the fittest' gene interpretation of evolution.

Science

Science is not an impersonal activity which can be detached from the human perspective: developments in quantum physics allow a much greater role for the human subject/subjectivity in exploring and developing our knowledgebase. Science is not the uncovering of regularities. It is much more complex and mysterious than that: scientific method also involves the use of 'meaning' and 'social collaboration' – these are empirically unobservable as entities, but they are integral in the practice of science itself. There is a distinction to be made between inert bodies and interpersonal interactions, but the fulcrum is not between 'science' and 'social interaction'. Rather, it is a question of which perspective to use to explore the undiscovered.

Faith

My own Christian faith is an active, inner, emotional and instinctive form of energy which I have striven to equalise with the more articulated and historical facts about Christ in the relevant literature. I have referred to some of these facts in an attempt to rebut the categorical conclusion some biologists have reached, namely that evolution has disproved the existence of God. Their assumptions that science is anti-subjective, physically generated alone, and removed from our own cognitive life are the ones I have tried to counteract. This piece of work, however, has not been an attempt to develop a phenomenology of faith based on the philosophical content of the essay: there is no mention of how the divine/human interaction might work, let alone how suffering can fit into a world created by a God whose character is good. I have striven to show that the power of the human mind in being able to artificially 'select', along with the limits of our understanding, reveal a different possibility to the atheistic idea that transcendent belief is dead.

Introduction

What is behind life itself – God, evolution or something else? Are we alone in this universe? How can we find out the reality? I am a retired social worker and teacher, now doing a small amount of care work and a lot of grandparenting. What do I know about it? If you read on, you will at least find out what I do know but of course, that may not help you.

When asking those questions, most people don't turn to philosophy. They often see philosophy as the province of intellectuals who basically speak a different language to the one of common sense. My friend, Ralph, who is very accomplished, said in a somewhat tongue-in-cheek way, "Isn't it a better use of time to put some shelves up?" I suppose when I took time out to study philosophy in more depth when I was much younger, if I am honest, it didn't really help me in my day to day life or in my relationships with other people, and it certainly has no relevance to putting up shelves. I began to enjoy philosophy and, now I have a little time, I have returned to it. Do I have a set of beliefs? I do, but I want this book to be read by those who are uncertain about any set of beliefs, whether connected to the primacy of science, religion or reason; later on, the substance of my faith will become clearer. I have tried to write it with as open a mind as possible, although it is perhaps only in the literary arts that a fuller escape from our own preconceptions is possible.

What fascinated me, and still does so, were the different places particular arguments can take us to; unearthing the assumptions behind particular standpoints deepens our understanding, sometimes by unpacking previously unspoken assumptions. Science, religion and reason are the three areas which this book focuses on. They are the precursors to those questions about equality, social justice, consumerism, environmentalism, diversity or nationalism, which are not covered here. That may be the ground of a further piece of study, something for my grandchildren to ponder when they have nothing better to do.

Why science, religion and reason? When going into some shops, there is background music. Our culture is a bit like that – there are various sounds and motifs which hum in the background. We have many such motifs: we are consumers, we have tolerance and we have the media. We also have science and religion. Somehow, we have difficulty putting them together. The philosopher Peter Winch puts it like this:

> On my view then, the philosophy of science will be concerned with the kind of understanding sought and conveyed by the scientist; the philosophy of religion will be concerned with the way in which religion attempts to present an intelligible picture of the world; and so on. And of course these activities and their aims will be mutually compared and contrasted. The purpose of such philosophical enquiries will be to contribute to our understanding of what is involved in the concept of intelligibility, so that we may better understand what it means to call reality intelligible.[1]

In other words, we have a desire to find the common theme from the different parts of our lives: in Winch's language this is what it

---

[1] *The Idea of a Social Science and its Relation to Philosophy*, page 20

means to make 'reality intelligible'. Evolution and religion have locked horns over recent years. That impasse has stopped some from seeing what evolution means for human beings, and also what belief in a creative God entails. For evolutionists, the original physicality of genetics has now become a subtler interplay between human choice and our DNA. For Christians, the idea of cause and effect has had to be redrawn as we find out more about the natural world. As modern neuroscience incorporates culture and human intention into its brief, the choice between atheism and faith is nowhere near as stark as it appeared to be even ten years ago. The mystery of how the mind and body intertwine is making us redefine what the mind is. Our ability to reason is both physical and, unless we are totally deceived by ourselves, autonomous. It's that ability to reason that stokes the fires of the humanist enlightenment. Is it strong enough to deliver a better world? Can we dispense with religion, or is it more complicated than that? Even if we could dispense with religion, would reason be able to marshal the force of human passions and our survival instinct in a way that protects everyone?

Evolutionists say that what is unknowable can become knowable, and that in itself dispels any need for a belief in God, whereas Christians might say that the character of God is only knowable through an active faith in Christ as God incarnate. Is there a parallel between solving a problem in a chemistry exam and resolving an argument with a friend? One is about pure reasoning and the other concerns a combination of reasons and feelings. Both evolution and faith have their presuppositions. For evolutionists, everything eventually has to be traced back to the survival of the species; for the Christian, what is ultimately left is one's inner connection with God, both here and beyond time. Philosophy does not help you to plump for one or another, but it does help you to appreciate how different views can be legitimately held. The language is technical, so I will begin with a brief attempt to describe the structure of this book in a straightforward way.

I start out exploring the question of what can be counted as true. Broadly speaking, I ask if experiential and interpersonal knowledge are just as valid as knowledge of scientifically observed physical processes. From this I move on to discuss the mind-body problem because even though we can and often do separate the physical from the mental aspects of life, there is no better meeting point of what is 'personal' and what is known as 'matter' than us, human beings. Our capacity to think then takes us to the issue of designing nature or for us, at least, redesigning it. Our ability to think creates as many problems as it solves, because so many different options are opened up. In the book, this ability to think is framed as a discussion about rationality, and later on reasoning. After assessing the suitability of the theory of evolution as an umbrella for all other theories, I look at the sceptical view of religion, exploring if it is a cause of human conflict or just one particular way we flawed human beings mistreat each other. Our perceptions of reason and science lead into a conclusion where what we *don't know* is as 'rational' a component of our understanding as what we *do know*. The purpose of the conclusion is to open up spaces for faith where previously some may have thought there weren't any.

The book is a journey. I started with what is now Chapter 7 and gradually found my way back to a starting point. From there I continued until I reached a stopping place at the end of Chapter 11. I hope that it is at least going to provoke a few thoughts, even if they are imaginative ones. Imagine, for example, that a theory is developed which links particle theory with what goes on in our minds when we make decisions. In particle theory there can be a whole range of potential outcomes, all of which are correct, although when observation is brought in, only one of those outcomes is detected. How might this affect our perception of what it is to make a decision?

There are a whole range of possible outcomes but in the end only one choice can be made. Despite the phenomenal growth in scientific knowledge over the last hundred years, we still find it difficult to really grasp the idea of a very large or even infinite set of outcomes. Is the idea of intelligence behind the universe more like a never-ending voyage of discovery rather than a step by step climb to the top of a mountain? Even if we cannot conceive of intelligence behind the universe, we should at least re-evaluate the balance between all the major scientific theories known to date. Along with the certainty that science brings comes a whole new set of questions with each new discovery. It is that balance between certainty and uncertainty which fine tunes our view of life and its origins.

September 2019

Chapter 1
What Do We Know?

The Traditional Model – All or Nothing?

> When we say 'that's the truth', what do we actually mean? Can we accidentally stumble across truth without realising it? Is there a difference between knowing something and proving a fact?

The notion of **truth** is central to any theory of knowledge. If I look at a mountain from one side, I cannot see it from the other side, so my view of it is limited to what *I can* see. When asking someone to marry me, I might think that they will say yes and I am taken aback when they refuse. My hopes are entirely subjective. If I conduct a scientific experiment, I may discover that the measurement of one factor negatively affects the measurement of another associated factor;[2] my presence in conducting the observation affects how much I am able to discover. Knowledge which is false cannot of course be counted as knowledge, but aside from that, our knowledge is partial – as there is always something more to be learnt – and so it could be argued that everything *we know* is to some extent subjective.

Alternatively, if we think that there is something objective 'out there' which we can call the truth, the realisation that we might either be

---

2. This is known as Heisenberg's uncertainty principle.

mistaken in our perceptions but accidentally correct, or have false beliefs which still lead us to the correct conclusion, means that *any* theory of knowledge is subject to conditions which cater for human error. I might be on a journey and lose my sense of direction but still by chance arrive at the correct destination. I might choose the wrong method in an exam but still somehow get the answer right. Edmund Gettier, Professor Emeritus at the University of Massachusetts Amherst, provides two formal examples which show that what we consider to be justified true belief can be wrong.[3] The basis of his examples was a conjunction of a near certainty with a random or unknown element; the outcome was that the random or unknown element materialised as true while the near certainty failed. From this he concluded that someone could arrive at the truth even though their initial belief about a near certainty was false.

Matthew Paisner in his 2012 paper, "Gettier and Justified True Belief", criticises Gettier for mistakenly suggesting that people "are possessed of discrete facts, each of which can be simply expressed in natural language and analysed separately".[4] We do not see facts in isolation. I believe that when I go to the cash point with my debit card and enter the correct details, I will gain access to my account. In doing so I am fulfilling certain conditions: first, I believe it, second, I consider it true because I have accessed cash before, and thirdly, it is justified because if one particular machine is not working, previous experience tells me that another one will. If the machine is malfunctioning, I do not say to myself that I will never try to access my account again on the basis that 'justified true belief' failed on one occasion. So, what is at stake is

---

[3.] These are the three essential elements of the traditional theory of knowledge. If something is to be counted as knowledge it must **not** be false – it must be accurate. There also must be reasons which support the assertion and those reasons are the justification for that particular piece of knowledge. Finally, if I am to count it as knowledge which I hold, I must believe it.

[4] Section 3 of the paper.

how we define knowledge; if we want to claim we have reached a point where it is impossible to contradict or amend a piece of knowledge, then Gettier has a point, as any claim that our knowledge is infallible is unsustainable. Alternatively, if we want to define knowledge as a 'good enough understanding' then the Gettier case of a mistaken belief being true is not strong enough for us to think that we are not in possession of any knowledge at all.[5]

Margarita Rosa Levin in her essay, "A Defence of Objectivity", says that the twentieth century which has "witnessed the greatest triumphs of science and technology" has also been "the century in which the ideal of objectivity has been subjected to the most severe challenges".[6] Despite this, she points out that "the idea that objectivity is not only possible but also regularly realized continues to underpin modern natural science".[7] Her principal argument is that it is essentially unreasonable to claim that there is no objective knowledge apart from the statement itself. In other words, to say there is no such thing as objectivity infers that the person making that claim can see everything.

Nevertheless, we cannot be sure if anything we think is the **absolute** truth. However, if we do say that the whole truth is beyond us, we do have to at least have an idea of what's missing in our own repertoire in relation to the truth. If pushed, philosophically speaking, we would need to identify what the requirements of actually knowing the truth would be. To claim that we have no purchase at all on the

---

5   Robert Nozik's rebuttal of the sceptical view that we cannot demonstrate that we truly know anything is debated in "The Possibility of Knowledge, Nozick and His Critics"(1987) Edited by Steven Luper-Foy, Rowman & Littlefield, New Jersey, USA.

6   "A Defence of Objectivity" from *The Theory of Knowledge, Classical and Contemporary Readings*, page 631

7   Ibid, page 631

truth does not explain the basis of social cooperation. Common agreements are necessary for society to function at all; something as simple as catching a bus depends on a common understanding of what buses do and can be used for. Is this worthy of attaching the label of 'truth' to? It is certainly the case that if people had a widely divergent understanding of what buses are and how to use them then the system would completely fail.

Secondly, as Levin states, the advances in applied science would not be possible without some grasp of the truth about the physical and natural world. Scientists make steps towards gaining the truth about certain conditions but do **not** claim to have reached a stage where no further knowledge is required. Levin says that those "who hold out for objective knowledge will argue that we can come to know some truths".[8] She accepts that there is a halfway position where we can claim there are truths, but also admits that we may not be in possession of some or all of them. This makes sense in that science gives us some grasp of nature, but scientific knowledge, at the same time, is provisional, constantly under scrutiny and revision. Take the following example reported by The Daily Telegraph's science editor, Sarah Knapton, on December 11th 2017:

> Huntington's disease patients have been offered new hope after a trial showed a ground breaking genetic treatment appears to slow down the illness ... Prof Sarah Tabrizi, director of University College London's Huntington's Disease Centre who led the phase 1 trial, said the results were 'beyond what I'd ever hoped,' and said it eventually may be possible to stop the disease before irreversible damage to the brain had occurred. (Knapton)

---

[8]   Ibid, page 641

It is important to note that Professor Tabrizi says it "eventually *may be possible* to stop the disease before irreversible damage to the brain had occurred" (emphasis added). If knowledge about genetic mutation in Huntingdon's sufferers can be tested, there is naturally caution about the efficacy and accuracy of those tests.

Having established that truth need not be an 'all or nothing' issue, it is also equally important to distinguish between the *authenticity* of subjective knowledge and the *validity* of scientific knowledge. Existentialism and phenomenology have brought our own self-awareness into focus,[9] while the natural sciences have emphasised the essential connection between assertion and evidence for a theory to be counted as knowledge. A complete theory of knowledge should account for both authenticity and validity and this chapter explores the tension between the two.

Validity and Endless Justification

Is all knowledge based on other supporting knowledge? Where does knowledge end? Could knowledge be never ending?

The epistemological theory of knowledge can be framed through the following question: how can we establish whether what we know is true?[10] Whenever we talk about the world around us, scientifically, we make propositions we believe to be true – for example, we might feel confident enough to say the Earth goes around the Sun. We justify this knowledge through providing evidence or relying on received

---

9   Existentialism focuses on the experience of being a living, feeling human being whilst phenomenology deals with how phenomena affect us.
10   Epistemological means the presuppositions, foundations, extent and validity issues applying to knowledge.

wisdom from the scientific community. That evidence, empirical or mathematical, is based on other kinds of knowledge, which in turn have to be justified to be considered true. Johannes Kepler's theory of planets having elliptical orbits rather than circular ones required specific knowledge of how to measure distance between stars and planets. This in turn depended on the accuracy of the instruments used, the information the eye sees and the ability of the brain to interpret it. Further to that is the underpinning assumption that the information processing carried out by the brain is not biased or predisposed to arrive at conclusions which mask the full reality. The core philosophical problem is that we are always referring on to further justifications of the knowledgebase. Even when we have established a consistent result, perhaps one confirmed independently by other factors, we cannot necessarily assume that there is nothing further to discover scientifically about a particular phenomenon.

This effectively brings into question whether we are locked into some kind of introspective spiral that is more about the way we 'see' the world as opposed to the way the world really is. This concern may be exaggerated because the world 'out there', of course, may **partially** resemble our perceptions.[11] The acceleration in the growth and application of scientific knowledge over the last 150 years nonetheless does suggest that our subjectivity has a foothold on knowledge about the external world. For any thinking creature with limited knowledge, justified **beliefs** are a requirement of learning because the territory being explored is unknown. Were we to have

---

[11] Max Velman's theory of "Reflective Monism" suggests our own sense of consciousness and the information processing mechanisms in our brains which facilitate our consciousness cannot be merged into a single methodology but as both stem from our evolutionary history, they do have the same source. Hence the link between neural mechanisms and our conscious understanding of them could mirror our partial understanding of the world 'out there'.

the absolute truth about some particular aspect of life, we would also have to be in possession of **all** knowledge, otherwise we might be missing a vital piece of information. Furthermore, if we postulate that we could eventually know everything, such a proposition entails the assumption that knowledge is finite. We have no way of knowing whether this is the case or not. Our own limitations have no bearing on this because it is quite possible that our own capacities are limited, whilst what there is to be known is unlimited. If numbers are infinite, why can't knowledge itself be? Ittay Weiss reported this in the I Newspaper on January 18th 2018:

> Prime numbers are more than just numbers that can only be divided by themselves and one. They are a mathematical mystery, the secrets of which mathematicians have been trying to uncover ever since Euclid proved that they have no end … An ongoing project – the Great Internet Mersenne Prime Search … recently discovered the largest prime number known to date. The number, simply written as 2 to the power of (77232917-1) was found by a volunteer who had dedicated 14 years to the endeavour. (Weiss)

The Logical Space of Reasons and Self-Knowledge

> Is knowledge only knowledge if you can explain it? Are my feelings part of what we can call the 'truth'?

One problem with the word 'justification' is that it can place a limiting condition on what knowledge can legitimately entail. Wilfrid Sellars said that to characterise "an episode or state of knowing, we are placing it in the logical space of reasons, of justifying and being able to justify what one says".[12] In other words, **unless** something can be articulated through language it should not be defined as knowledge. The capacity to test for repetition or variation of the conditions which explain the particular subject in question is seen as essential and cannot be done without language. On this account, knowledge must be refined and challenged in order to improve its accuracy. It seems absolutely reasonable to place knowledge into the realm of openminded enquiry rather than immovable dogmatism. The logical space of reasons as justification implies the capacity to **convince** others of the strength of an argument. It is of course possible to convince oneself of something,[13] but it must eventually be articulated, recordable and open to others to develop further, at least in principle.

So, in limiting the definition of knowledge to that which is explainable and justifiable in the context of human enquiry, we may preserve a sense of consideration of all possible options, but are we **also** unwittingly limiting the scope of knowledge in so doing? To be more precise, can non-epistemic experience be counted as knowledge? Even if a particular experience can be described with words, the description cannot give us full access to the experience in question. This is not to say that the raw material of our senses and feelings do not interact with and influence the conceptual aspects of our minds, and vice versa.[14] The question is whether a feeling or

---

[12] *Empiricism and the Philosophy of Mind*, page 76

[13] Ludwig Wittgenstein's objection to private language is that there is no way anyone else could know what a person meant if they had never had exposure to others in forming concepts in the first place.

[14] This account sidesteps the debate as to whether there are perceptual experiences which are completely immune from conceptual explanation, a view known as foundationalism. A critical summary of Foundationalism can be found at https://plato.stanford.edu/

sensation which we can only partly describe to a third party should count as knowledge.[15]

Furthermore, the concept of 'truth' itself is not easy to pin down. Criminal courts are concerned whether something is true or false. This kind of truth is about establishing the facts of a situation. Someone deciding whether to commit themselves to a long-term relationship may ask themselves if their feelings are true. This kind of truth involves introspection to try and discover the core of what one person feels for another and how genuine those feelings are. A scientist exploring genetic mutation will be exploring DNA patterns in retrospect to see how they have changed through highly technical methods of exploring biological samples. This kind of truth is about discovering hitherto unknown physical processes.

So the facts of a crime, the feelings in a relationship and the mechanics of genetic mutation are all subject to the word 'truth', but the idea that all of these can be tested with equal force and in the same way is untenable. We can test for the effect of magnetic fields repeatedly, but we cannot rerun the argument we had with a family member last week as if it had never happened. Yet it would be absurd to claim that the argument was outside the legitimate field of our knowledge. Self-knowledge is relational, unique and, in terms of the experience itself, **unrepeatable**. Nevertheless, it is something we **know**, namely, how we experience ourselves. It is still 'knowledge'.[16]

---

[15] To cite a famous example, the court could not decide whether OJ Simpson murdered his wife or not.

[16] This is a contentious point with those who consider self-knowledge to be "subjective" and therefore not necessarily part of a wider constituency of truth from which knowledge is derived. This in turn creates the unforeseen implication that all such "subjective knowledge" cannot be included in any account of objective knowledge; however, any account of "objective" or externalist knowledge as it is known must be able to explain the nature and cause of subjective and potentially inaccurate judgements.

We are just less certain as to what methodology to use in exploring personal knowledge compared to the methodologies used in the natural sciences where *repetition* is an essential part of the process through which theory becomes knowledge.

The Passions – a Paradigm of Authenticity

> How can I research my own feelings? Can scientific methods help me?

Even though they are not easily amenable to laboratory testing, our own experiences can be said to be the *most reliable* form of self-knowledge we have. 'I feel tired' is true, provided I am being honest. Regardless of whether I articulate or simply sense that I am tired, for me it is true; I do not need to use a further context to justify my sense of tiredness. This is in line with David Hume's contention that all our thinking ultimately stems from sensations. His position is not that every thought has an origin in a felt experience, but that complex thinking can be traced back to simple ideas which have their origins in the sensations we have.[17]

Experiencing anger, for example, has and needs no frame of reference to evidence it in the same way an acid/alkaline test does with a piece of litmus paper. It is self-evident to me that I am angry. My friend might sense a change in my mood, even if I tell myself and him that I am not angry, that feeling of repressed anger will still be mine and mine alone. In general, we tend to be more certain about the validity of our own feelings as opposed to working out what other people are feeling. If I participate in a psychological research study, the researchers might look at a variety of physiological, relational,

---

[17] To see the original explanation, go to *A Treatise of Human Nature*, Penguin Classics, London, page 461.

social status and other factors, and they might have some success in predicting certain outcomes or even methods of anger management, but they will **not be able to experience** what I experienced. The prediction will refer to the likelihood of particular behaviours and the factors contributing to it. Hume's analysis of how reasons superimpose themselves on passions and adjust them appears to be very pertinent for the researcher. So the principle of induction does not apply to human emotions in the same way it does to the litmus paper test.[18] Every time I do the litmus paper test, the result should be broadly the same. When I am angry today, a psychologist researching into my anger cannot feel the same anger in two weeks' time.

The principle of induction is based on constant repetition of the original event under the same conditions. How can this apply to an individual's feelings at a particular moment in time? The art of theatre and the practice of empathy are the closest we get to understanding someone's feelings, but this is not mathematical or experimental, it is expressive and relational. Attempts at recreation vary in their authenticity, but they are possible. However, human passion cannot be calibrated in the same way a litmus paper test can. The difficulty lies in the idea of measurement. Measuring the intensity of feelings on a numerical scale is not the same as experiencing the feeling. Feelings are not units and so any measurement of them affects their true nature. If I am angry and then I'm asked to rank it on various scales by a psychologist, that helps the psychologist and I place the feeling

---

18 Induction is where, after many instances of A following B, it is certain the next time A occurs, B will follow. Bertrand Russell, in his famous *History of Western Philosophy*, says, "If this principle (namely the principle of induction) is not true, every attempt to arrive at general scientific laws from particular observations is fallacious, and Hume's scepticism is inescapable for an empiricist". page 612

into a framework. My original feeling of anger was unmeasurable at the time. To genuinely replicate it means that it would have to be **unmeasurable again**.

So far, the discussion has centred on the issue of what it is to 'know', rather than 'who' is doing the knowing. The knowing element focuses on truth, justification and belief, but even if those elements were to be safely secured, the theory of knowledge falters if the holder of the knowledge is a fragile, changeable and ultimately indefinable nonentity.

The Problem of Identity

Am I in a position to hold knowledge, or am I a mixture of experiences and sensations which add up to me calling myself 'me' just to get through life?

At this point, Hume's bundle theory of the self becomes relevant because it follows a similar methodology to the evolutionary approach, starting from the simplest and earliest beginnings and moving on to more complex mechanisms. He considers, in short, that personal identity is the result of a collection of sensations which each individual experiences:

For my part, when I enter most intimately into what I call myself, I always stumble on some particular perception or other, of heat or cold, light or shade, love or hatred, pain or pleasure. I never can catch myself at any time without a perception and never can observe anything but the perception. When my perceptions are removed for any time, as by sound sleep, so long am I insensible of myself and may truly be said not to exist ... But setting aside some metaphysicians of this kind (i.e. those who maintain there is something called a real self) I venture to affirm to the rest of mankind, that they are nothing but a bundle or collection of different perceptions, which succeed each other with inconceivable rapidity, and are in a perpetual flux and movement.[19]

For Hume, there is no real entity called 'me', it is an ensemble of parts interacting with each other. If that is the case, philosophically speaking, then the phrase 'I know' has no real basis. Whereas before it had no basis because of the way emotion confuses knowledge, here it has no basis because there is no genuine place or person to 'hold' it. The two prongs of Hume's argument are linked because if all our reasoning can be traced back to our sensations, then our understanding of **who** we are also derives from that **same** range of sensations. After all, the realisation that we are individuals takes place when we are very young and seems to emerge from a plethora of emotions, both pleasurable and painful, from before we are one year old. This perspective suggests that what happens as we grow older is simply a more sophisticated version of our early development. The notion of growth from a purely physical beginning into an entity called the self which has a life of its own is, for Hume, a mistake. This approach has a certain brutal logic to it, but the exercise of science requires a purposeful self, i.e. intentionality. This does not mean that the idea of personal identity is impregnable against manipulation or self-deception or even total disintegration – those with extreme mental health conditions experience this kind of internal collapse. However, because intentionality is essential for the exercise of scientific enquiry, the question arises as to whether intentionality is possible without the self. If rationality is the intention to do what I

---

[19]   *A Treatise of Human Nature*, page 300

think I ought to do, it makes no sense to write the sentence without the 'I': 'to do what think ought to do' is the result. If we are capable of intentional action, then we are also agents of that intentionality.

Scientific Laws – Are They Universal?

> Even if I am confident that I am a reliable holder of information, can I be sure that there is some knowledge which is always true in all circumstances?

Hume maintained that because A has always followed B, it does not follow that it **always** will. He was attacking the principle that scientific laws could be discovered through experimental methods where consistently similar outcomes were obtained. Perhaps the emergence of Stephen Hawking's Big Bang theory has given Hume more credence than he had previously received.

Stephen Hawking, in his 2005 lecture 'The Origin of the Universe', explained where Einstein's General Law of Relativity breaks down.[20] When the universe was very young, the structure of matter was compressed and subject to very strong gravitational forces. In these conditions, explanations from quantum theory take over from the general theory of relativity.

In saying that there is a point where one scientific theory takes over from another, i.e. quantum theory from the general theory of relativity, Hawking is perhaps unwittingly agreeing with Hume that scientific 'laws' do not apply in all cases. He is not, however, rejecting the principle of induction, which is as vital to the emergence of the

---

[20] Hawking, S, (2005) 'The Origin of the Universe': *http://www.hawking.org.uk/ the-origin-of-the* universe.html For copyright reasons, I am summarising relevant parts of this lecture.

Big Bang theory as it is to the theory of evolution.[21] Using the Big Bang theory as an example, evidence of an expanding universe and fainter and fainter radiation waves are tied together to imply that the universe itself, including time and space, had a starting point. Hawking explains this as space/time having a beginning at a point where matter has an infinite density. At the edge of scientific endeavour lies unknowns about the way theories apply, and so induction in terms of a particular context may not apply in *all* contexts. Marcus du Sautoy summarises the current state of knowledge about time in the following way:

> Understanding the nature of time before the Big Bang was another edge that I thought was unassailable. But chinks have opened up in that wall too. Recent progress has provided us with ways to theorize and even perhaps detect evidence of a time before we thought it all began. And yet the question of whether time had a beginning or extends infinitely into the past feels like one that will remain on the scientific books for some time yet.[22]

Science cannot work without the principle of induction because without it, regularities are impossible to identify. We say there are

---

[21]   The theory of evolution can be characterised as consisting of random genetic mutation, time as measured by the calendar year system, and the natural selection of genes which adapt to environmental changes. Species developments are matched against fossil evidence as well as other research tools, for example, studying the behaviour of bacteria (some have a very short life span). Genetic mutations over many generations can be observed and compared to mutations in other species. The principle of induction applies because the process of evolution in some species is held to apply to all species even if the specific linking evidence is yet to be unearthed.

[22]   *What We Cannot Know*, page 407

universal laws under certain sets of conditions. However, when those conditions change, the same laws will not necessarily apply and, as du Sautoy suggests, those former laws are not overtaken by another neat framework. We are travelling into the unknown. There is one factor which is no longer the immovable constant it was when the *Origin of Species* was published in the mid-19th century. 'Time' is no longer a fixed universal calibration, and so the scientific theories which depend on it will inevitably become more limited in their scope.

Concluding Remark

> Does it make sense to research a historical event in the same way we explore the physical world around us? Should we be surprised if scientific methods do not tell us everything about how our emotions, feelings and thoughts work?

Hubble's law, which is completely reliant on observation, can be tested again and again. However, the French Revolution only happened once. It cannot be repeated and so can only be explored through tracing a variety of information sources such as literature, family histories or fashions in art and architecture at the time. If we could understand the French Revolution by repeatedly experiencing it over and over again, we would no doubt take advantage of this to gain more insight. If we were to truly understand it from the perspectives of *all* who were involved, we would have to repeat it over and over again, 'Groundhog Day' style.[23] It would be a dream come true for historians and psychologists alike. It seems more than counterintuitive to think

---

[23]   'Groundhog Day' was a film where a suitor was repeatedly given the opportunity to live through the same day until he was able to convince the girl of his dreams to become romantically involved with him.

we could use the way we explore our own feelings and emotions to discover more about the velocity of galaxies. Likewise, the velocity of galaxies leaves us cold when it comes to exploring the depths of our emotional and relational life. It may, of course, feel more 'objective' to reclassify our feelings as less important than cold hard knowledge of the universe gained through recent scientific enterprise, but what we are in fact comparing is the relative success of at least two different methodologies.

In conclusion, the nature of the evidence and the methods of testing are fundamentally different between history and scientific laws which are dependent on empirical findings. Hence it is much easier to authenticate 'what I felt', but much harder, and some would say impossible, to test those feelings by replicating the experience.[24] Conversely, validating physical processes in laboratories or through mathematical calculation is easier when the observer does not interfere with the experimental conditions. This may not be as straightforward as it sounds.

Our minds, however, are the 'spaghetti junction' of physiology and neural pathways, cognitive activity, language, feelings and spiritual inclinations. A key debate over which of these is the prevalent influence amongst these has been conducted through what is known as the mind-body debate. It is this debate I turn to in the next chapter.

---

[24] Some psychotherapists would disagree with this contention.

Chapter 2
The Mind-Body Debate

If there is such a thing as knowledge, how do our minds retain it?

In the first chapter, we explored whether our self-knowledge counts as the most genuine kind of knowledge even though it is very difficult to reproduce our interpersonal relationships in a laboratory research context. Knowledge is held in our brains and from then on it can travel into the various channels that humans have devised to remember, record and store knowledge. One of the key issues philosophers and thinkers have wrestled with, from early times, is how our minds actually work. Today neuroscience is at the forefront of this enquiry.

A Historical U-turn

In early times the mind was seen as non-physical, so why have we changed our approach so dramatically in the modern era? Is it because modern approaches argue that thinking has its roots in biology?

From very early recorded Greek philosophy, the pre-eminence of the mind over body, as in Plato's Forms and Aristotle's active reasoning, reflected the higher status of thought over matter. Plato's view was that as human beings we find ourselves inside a mixture of simple mathematical structures, imperfect ideas and a disordered material universe. Erik Ostenfield says that, for Plato, the "body and its constituents do not deserve the name of cause".[25] Where the split between human reality and another realm comes is with Plato's Forms; in short, these are perfect ideas which are real and exist independently of us. Human beings experience fragments of these perfect ideas and have the means to experience them fully, eventually through the immortality of the soul.

For Aristotle, although he felt that Form is integrated into nature rather than removed from it as Plato maintained, he argued for a different separation, one between active and passive reason. Human beings possess something called passive reason which is brought to life by its perfect external counterpart. Ostenfield puts it like this: "the active intellect is *both* in the soul and separable (*choristos*) and assumed not only to exist after death (*choritheis*) but indeed to be external and ever thinking".[26]

For both Plato and Aristotle, the critical point was in the inference of perfection in intelligible reality as opposed to the imperfection in human understanding. It was not between mind and matter; it was about the potential power of thought as an absolute against the mediocrity and imprecision in human cognition.

It is not possible here to trace the development of philosophical thought from Plato and Aristotle to the present day in any meaningful way, but it is important to note that there are significant landmarks in 16th and 17th century writings which form the 'runway' from which modern biological explanations of cognition have taken off.[27] Baruch Spinoza and René Descartes took very different views of the

---

25   *Ancient Greek Psychology and the Modern Mind-Body Debate*, page 33

26   Ibid, page 46

27   A. C. Grayling's *The History of Philosophy* (2019) is the most recent summary of the way philosophy has moved throughout the centuries.

distinction between the mind and the body.[28] Daniel Dennett explains how Descartes "thought that all human minds were wonderful, capable of feats that no mere animal could match, feats that were beyond the reach of any imaginable *mechanism*, however elaborate and complicated. So he concluded that minds ... were not material entities like lungs or brains, but made of some second kind of stuff that didn't have to obey the laws of physics".[29] (emphasis original)

Spinoza, whose lifetime crossed over with Descartes, departed from his view in a very radical way, claiming that mind and body were simply different expressions of the same substance. This was not a view held by the establishment but gained ground from the 17th century onwards so that today communication is seen as an *evolved* function formed through its biological antecedents. In his paper concerning the evolution of primate communication and metacommunication, Joelle Proust explains the pathway from basic nonverbal cues through to exchanging information with others where there is no immediate environmental stimulus:[30]

First, the function of communication *evolved* from more or less inflexible, recurrent signalling, to flexible communication. Hence, whereas coding-decoding processes merely involve associations between cues, extracting a message content across contexts of production requires complex inferential abilities. Second, such flexibility is rooted in a properly human function: to deliberately exchange information in the context of *cooperative action*.[31] (emphasis added)

---

[28] Descartes lived from 1596-1650, Spinoza lived from 1632-1677.
[29] *From Bacteria to Bach and Back*, pages 13-14
[30] This paper contains a comprehensive overview of the current work in relation to communication in non-human species.
[31] *Mind and Language, Vol 31, No 2*, page 178

The various types of communication – from signalling to shared knowledge of alarm calls, from recognising emotions in specific contexts to using language in novel situations – are now all part of human capability. Proust's evolutionary arguments "for defending continuity" are firstly that humans possess the entire communication repertoire just listed, and secondly, that there is "similarity between nonverbal signals of satisfaction" for both primates and young children.[32] The idea of capacities that humans share with a vast range of other species supports the modern view that what we call 'mind' is derived from a long evolutionary history, which began with purely physical interactions.[33]

Imagine we had no recourse to articulate our feelings in the spoken word. In the face of danger, we could still look at each other and know we had to do something to counteract it. Such interaction would amount to a shared intention. This is a capacity in apes which Proust refers to.[34] To move to human language from this point is the basis of the evolutionary case. Our perceptual sensing mechanisms, referred to by Proust as "affordance sensing", concerning what may or may not be to our benefit, could be the precursors of language capacity.[35]

---

[32] Ibid, page 179

[33] Evolutionary biologists are in accord with Hume's perspective that mental events are representations of sensations. Hume's contention that predictive laws are not sustainable because repeated events do not mean that they will always continue to be repeated, also sits well with the idea of natural selection. It does not sit so well with the idea that as one layer of communicative competence (impulsive) is overlaid by another (habitual) it will then be automatically overlaid by yet another (strategic). See Proust for this scheme, pages 180-181.

[34] *Mind and Language, Vol 31, No 2*, page 188

[35] Ibid, page 185. For a fuller discussion of affordances see page 189 of Proust's article, where he outlines the different contexts in which we experience affordance sensing: environmental, the sharing of emotions, the need to communicate and the demands for more information (epistemic).

The Modern Context

> The mind is now seen as inseparable from the body, but to what extent are we really in control of ourselves particularly as brain research progresses? How are our emotions tied up with our thinking?

The key issue around the mind-body debate has historically been about the metaphysical assumptions behind each camp. For those who consider the mental and spiritual dimensions of life to be of ultimately the greatest significance, the merger of cognitive capacities into evolutionary history is inadequate as an explanation of human experience. In contrast, those who consider transcendent immanence to be a fanciful impossibility prefer the evidence-based physical explanations of mental functioning, in the positivist traditions of 20th century British philosophy. For evolutionary biologists, the distinction between mind and body is an inheritance from the past which is now invalid.

The debate about who is in charge, your brain or 'you', still continues. Raymond Tallis and David Eagleman bring the arguments into a modern context. Tallis' argument is based around the huge increase in knowledge about matching neural activity with mental events, whereas Eagleman questions whether this means we are automatons, implying that culture is excluded by the focus on individual brain mechanisms. Tallis responds by saying that his book is not written by an automaton but that we give insufficient weight to the predispositions set down in our brains together with the work the brain does *without* our conscious awareness. Eagleman does not believe this is a sufficient rationale for the growth of scientific knowledge; if our conscious awareness is the tip of an iceberg over which we have no control, he questions how we could have learnt so much about ourselves and the natural world.[36]

Antonio Domasio provides a very relevant context to the polemic between Eagleman and Tallis by showing how both our emotional inheritance and our experiences underpin our cerebral competence. In his book *Looking For Spinoza*, he describes how memories are triggered, how they are connected to past personal experience and add up to the accumulated species specific genetic inheritances we have: "eventually, in a fruitful combination with past memories, imagination, and reasoning, feelings led to the emergence of foresight and the possibility of creating novel, non-stereotypical responses".[37] Emotions are integral to cognitive functioning: without this underpinning memory of emotionally triggered experience, cognitive functioning becomes unhinged from the reality of human interaction.[38]

It is as if Domasio is pointing out that the opposition between neurology and autonomy is oversimplified because our cognitive capacities are linked to our *personal* evolutionary histories: the memories and emotions we have form the basis of our individual cognitive capabilities. There must be a huge range of variation between individuals. The combination of what lies in each unique brain, our ability to influence others and most importantly our ability to innovate, is too complex to unravel into a species-wide solvable equation between genetic predisposition and human autonomy. The combination of evolution, emotion and cognition are the building

---

[36]   This debate was reported on the Guardian website on 29th April 2012

[37]   *Looking For Spinoza, Joy, Sorrow and the Feeling Brain*, page 80

[38]   Domasio demonstrates that when the relevant emotional responses are separated from cognitive activity through brain injuries, patients who can solve hypothetical problems are completely at a loss when faced with similar situations in reality. You can find his explanation on pages 141-4 in *Looking For Spinoza*.

blocks of culture, not the outcomes. However, what he does add to the Tallis-Eagleman debate is that the exercise of autonomy and the influence of culture over time become embedded into our neurological memories.

The key conceptual question is how a complex physical system can realise genuine autonomy. While artificial intelligence research involves seeking to design machines that can think for themselves, we are still trying to puzzle out what the neurological constituents, combinations and connections which allow us to think, record and interact are. Of course, the two may be connected. The search is still on for the connections between neural patterns and neural imaging, as well as the general search for integrated neurophysiological answers to decision making.[39]

If a mechanistic rather than organic view of the brain is assumed, the goals of research are adjusted accordingly. For example, Dennett suggests that human brains are the "only brains so far seriously infected with memes".[40] A meme is "an element of culture that may be considered to be passed on by non-genetic means".[41] He compares cultural memes to viruses that get into the system – they are just there rather than needing to be understood before they are allowed into our minds.[42] In his words, "human comprehension – and approval – is neither necessary nor sufficient for the fixation of a meme in a culture".[43] It is clear that if this view of cognition is accepted, then research aims will be focussed on neural associations rather than mechanisms which explain how innovation occur.

---

[39]   See page 198 of Domasio's *Looking for Spinoza* for details.
[40]   *From Bacteria to Bach and Back*, page 174
[41]   Ibid, page 209
[42]   Ibid, page 173
[43]   Ibid, page 211

All neurological activity does not have to be deterministic but can configure to allow for genuine decision making. Even from a lay point of view, it seems possible to conceive of option A in a decision-making process as one neural configuration of information, memory and emotional tapestry, whilst option B is another different neural configuration of the same elements. Then, one can speculate that another complementary neural competence is the ability to compare A with B. Here is the neural basis, at least in theory, of a reasoning and decision-making process.

Whether one adopts the former or the latter approach, the solution sought after is to uncover specific concrete information. However, it must be asked: can everything be pinned down in specific terms?

The Unknown

What can we say about what we don't know?

For the evolutionist, one cannot know in advance how random selection will proceed, so this knowledge is retrospective – that means predictive knowledge for that process is, at least in principle, unreachable.[44] Could it be that we also cannot predict what decision I might make on a particular date two years from now? We may know what an individual's brain will do if decision A is selected and also what it will do if decision B is selected, but this alone will **not** tell us what that individual might do **in advance**. If there are a variety of possible outcomes which the brain could configure at some point in the future, is prediction of what those configurations might be beyond our grasp? As uncertainty is inbuilt into species development,

---

[44] Random selection here must be truly random and not just a smokescreen for an undiscovered theory.

is freedom of choice neurologically built into our minds?[45] If that freedom is genuine freedom, a whole range of potential outcomes must be present when the particular choice is made.

If not being able to predict everything is one type of unknown, the essence of a thought or series of ideas is another potential mystery. Can I invite you to take a leap of imagination into the very distant future and use your abstract thinking powers? One day, the Sun will burn out. Consider the notion that at that time no record exists of Shakespeare's work and no living creature retains any memory of his plays.

There are three options:

a) The works of Shakespeare *never* existed – this is plainly not true.

b) The works of Shakespeare *once* existed but no longer do – this is the materialist account. I cannot see them, remember them or read them.

c) The works of Shakespeare were once configured by a creative mind (Shakespeare), so even though they no longer exist materially or in memory, should the ideas and narrative in them be thought of and written again by someone else, they would not be entirely original. If such a recreation is feasible, where do the original ideas lie if they have no material resting place?

---

[45] I am not talking about probabilities established through psychological and sociological research, but exact prediction in individual cases. Additionally, this does not rule out the influence of external factors; for a philosophical account of such influences see Nanay, B (February 2016) 'The Role of Imagination in Decision Making', *Mind and Language*, Vol. 31 No. 1, page 130.

This is entirely different from saying because you can conceive of the works of Shakespeare they necessarily exist, which was St. Anslem's ontological argument about God – it is to say that once the an idea has been conceived, no materialistic process can unwind history to say that a particular idea can never be revived, even if all physical traces of it have been destroyed. The nature of thought has a mysterious quality which is hard to quantify in the modern context of evidence-based neurology.

This may appear to be a thinly veiled attempt to introduce the idea of transcendence into a hard-edged scientific discussion, but it is not just faith-based religions which employ the notion of non-physical entities. Dennett's description of memes has already been noted and Carl Jung's notion of the collective unconscious is another example. The collective unconscious, for Carl Jung, is the commonly shared human inheritance accumulated from the time our species emerged, an ancestral memory that has no obvious physical basis.

Concluding Remark

> Is reality greater than any one factor which contributes to our capacity to think and decide?

Domasio's telling phrase explains the dilemma from an evolutionary perspective: "Nature lacks a plan for human flourishing, but nature's humans are allowed to devise such a plan." [46] It seems that whatever the balance between predisposition and genuine human innovation, the scales are not tipped in favour of the overwhelming imprint of memes onto our minds as Dennett makes out. Neurobiological

---

[46] *Looking for Spinoza*, page 287

research embraces the concept of free choice *within* the workings of the brain, not outside of it. Form *is* embodied in matter, but not dominated by it. This is because the beginnings of life inherently have the **potential** ingredients of intelligent design, as Domasio explains in *The Strange Order of Things*:

> When a living organism behaves intelligently and winningly in a social setting, we assume that the behaviour results from foresight, deliberation, complexity, all with the help of a nervous system. It is now clear, however, that such behaviours could also have sprung from the bare and spare equipment of a single cell, namely in a bacterium, at the dawn of the biosphere. 'Strange' is too mild a word to describe this reality.[47]

The brain *is* capable of intentional decision making, not as a machine but as part of being a human being. The body and brain include the ability to make genuine choices within the context of predispositions accumulated through evolutionary history. Decisions are not purely the product of selective non-physical memes which we are unaware of. For a species to have evolved which can research, and to some extent, reshape its own physiology, means the power of thought is immense. Our emotions, our experience, our genetics and our culture all contribute to who we are, but to try and use any one of those factors as a peephole into the entirety of life does not provide a full enough picture of reality. We can and should seek to evaluate the balance of the empirical, the unknown, the relational and the mysterious in our quest to make reality intelligible.

---

[47]   *The Strange Order of Things,* page 6

Chapter 3
Our Capacity for Intelligent Redesign

Is the idea of an intelligent designer made redundant by the theory of evolution?

The mind-body debate as presented in the previous chapter does not dismiss the idea of an intelligent creator, because within evolution itself lies the potential for cognitive creative capacity. So, it is *not* an upward journey from the foundation stone of materialism to a superstructure of cognition (mirrored in spiritual terms as moving away from transcendence towards an earth-bound immanence) but rather a question of cognition, creativity and materialism all being interconnected. Whether or not there is an intelligent designer behind the natural world, therefore, remains an open question, even though such a possibility does not easily resonate with the agnostic instincts held by many. In the same way science cannot explain away religion, neither can religion explain away science.

Darwin's Legacy

There is a difference between Darwin's approach to the idea of an intelligent Creator and the approach some of his supporters have taken. Darwin was far less categorical in his condemnation of the idea. Why might this be?

Charles Darwin did not rule out the notion of a creative intelligent force, but his views did change over time from theism to agnosticism. His writings may have suggested a close alliance with Herbert Spencer, but his true feelings were more accurately reflected in his autobiographical notes. In fact, he distanced himself from Spencer. It is clear that when Darwin wrote the *Origin of Species* it was not intended to alter anyone's belief in God: his subsequent doubts and fluctuations demonstrate that he did not regard his theory as a proof against God's existence. He was very aware of the significance of human cognitive capability, as this famous passage in his autobiography illustrates:

> Another source of conviction in the existence of God, connected with the reason and not with the feelings, impresses me as having much more weight. The extreme difficulty or rather impossibility of conceiving this immense and wonderful universe, including man with his capacity of looking far backwards and far into futurity, as the result of blind chance or necessity. When thus reflecting I feel compelled to look to a First Cause having an intelligent mind in some degree analogous to that of man; and I deserve to be called a Theist. This conclusion was strong in my mind about the time, as far as I can remember, when I wrote the *Origin of Species*; and it is since that time that it has very gradually with many fluctuations become weaker.[48]

More and more doubts crept into Darwin's thinking as he grew older particularly about the doctrine of hell as well as the 'design'

---

[48]   *The Autobiography of Charles Darwin, 1809-1882*, pages 92-93

element in the natural world; he was, however, taken by the moral teaching outlined in the Gospels. Nevertheless, in letter to John Fordyce on 7th May 1879, Darwin wrote:

> In my most extreme fluctuations I have never been an Atheist in the sense of denying the existence of a God. I think that generally (and more and more as I grow older), but not always, that an Agnostic would be the more correct description of my state of mind.(Darwin Correspondence Project)[49]

There is a major and very marked contrast between Darwin's personal views and what is known today as Darwinism. Ernst Mayr interpreted the implications of Darwin's views in the following way at a conference in Stockholm in 1999:

> Darwinism rejects all supernatural phenomena and causations. The theory of evolution by natural selection explains the adaptedness and diversity of the world solely materialistically. It no longer requires God as creator or designer (although one is certainly still free to believe in God even if one accepts evolution) … Eliminating God from science made room for strictly scientific explanations of all natural phenomena; it gave rise to positivism; it produced a powerful intellectual and spiritual revolution, the effects of which have lasted to this day.[50](Mayr)

---

[49] This is Letter no.12041 held by the Darwin Correspondence Project at https://www.darwinproject.ac.uk/letter/DCP-LETT-12041.xml

[50] Mayr, E, "Darwin's Influence on Modern Thought." Scientific American, 2009, *https://www.scientificamerican.com/article/darwins-influence-on-modern-thought/* (Accessed 28 May 2017) This article is based on the September 23, 1999, lecture that Mayr delivered in Stockholm on receiving the Crafoord Prize from the Royal Swedish Academy of Science.

Even Mayr's universal application of evolutionary theory still offers the option of believing in God even though it is clear that Mayr himself feels no further explanation is required.[51] This latter position was adopted by both Darwin's contemporaries and successors: two examples follow.

Evolution as a Wider Explanation of Human Relations – Three Implications

What are the implications of adopting the theory of evolution as a model for society to follow?

Darwin's contemporary, Herbert Spencer, wrote extensively as to how societies are similar to living organisms: the interconnectedness of their functions resembles the way the organs in our bodies are reliant on one another. He used the biological model of species development to explain human behaviour and believed the discovery of natural selection to be so fundamental that it had to be ***the*** template for understanding human relationships. This trend has continued into many modern psychological approaches, as well as a general Zeitgeist that is part and parcel of today's culture. Ernst Mayr again summarises the contemporary approach:

Natural selection, applied to social groups, is indeed sufficient to account for the origin and maintenance of altruistic ethical systems; cosmic teleology, an intrinsic process leading life

---

[51] In contrast Dennis Alexander, Director of the Faraday Institute for Science and Religion, St. Edmund's College, Cambridge has written an account explaining why Christians should accept evolution as a biological theory which illustrates God's creation. 'Creation or Evolution – Do We Have To Choose?' (2014)

automatically to ever greater perfection, is fallacious, with all seemingly teleological phenomena explicable by purely material processes; and determinism is thus repudiated, which places our fate squarely in our own evolved hands.(Mayr)

Mayr is saying that there is no overall plan in nature, but we humans can now determine our own destiny. Our fate is placed "squarely in our own evolved hands".(Mayr) The morphing of biological modelling into purposeful control contradicts a key feature of evolutionary species development which is inherently haphazard and completely unpredictable. So human dominance over other species has come about through natural selection, while our recent 'promotion', allowing us to determine our own fate, has made our future vulnerable. This means that all postulations about kin loyalty, the value of altruism or human autonomy may be completely mistaken if homo sapiens eventually dies out: this could be in favour of another species or simply a case of self-destruction.

Anné Verhoef, a contemporary writer on religious development, reinforces Mayr's progression in explaining why human beings can take over from evolutionary processes in order to live meaningful lives.

In the science-religion discourse, particularly as discussed by Cornel du Toit, religion is understood as a product of normal evolutionary processes and is therefore natural, although most religions are characterised by faith in the supernatural. The supernatural can, however, be discarded, because human beings no longer need supernatural powers to explain the cosmos and live meaningful lives.[52]

---

[52]   *Acta Academia, Vol 45,No 4,* page 177

A steady state is assumed: by implication, Verhoef is adopting Spencer's use of evolution as a **complete** theory from which other aspects of living can be derived. However, according to the theory of evolution, the matter of whether belief in a transcendent God is an advantage to our species or not, can only be analysed retrospectively. Firstly, we need to know if a few hundred years of **not** believing is long enough to make judgements about species advantage: this is difficult to assess in a world with so much cultural and religious variation. Any set of beliefs has to ultimately translate into genetic structure and even if this is possible, we would need to know what timescale to use. Very little time has elapsed since the publication of the *Origin of Species* and it is uncertain whether we have the appropriate knowledge to know what 'timepiece' is appropriate. Dawkins' summary of relevant timescales in *The Greatest Show on Earth* does **not include** the translation of belief into our genetic structure:

> For evolutionary purposes, clocks that can measure centuries or perhaps decades are about the fastest we need. This fast end of the spectrum of natural clocks – tree rings and carbon dating – is useful for archaeological purposes, and for dating specimens on the sort of timescale that covers the domestication of the dog or the cabbage. At the other end of the scale, we need natural clocks that can time hundreds of millions, even billions of years.[53]

Secondly, Verhoef's statement implies that humanity can move forward in some kind of purposeful direction without the notion of a transcendent God. Even without the religious element, the concept

---

[53]   *The Greatest Show on Earth, The Evidence for Evolution,* pages 87-88

of 'moving forward' is contestable. Take, for example, the notion of living in a society which is fully just and fair; is it an evolutionary advantage to pursue such ambitions even though we know no such society can ever exist? An answer might be that a society without aspiration will fall into inertia, regardless of whether equality of dignity, health and opportunity can ever be realised. Is it a fiction worth pursuing because, in evolutionary terms, such goals will enhance cooperation within our species? Conversely, repugnant as it is, from a perspective which seeks to enhance species fitness, brutal regimes improve the chances of human survival in the long run because they focus on potential threats to their societies as a whole. Social justice improves social cohesion whilst xenophobic dictatorship improves defensive awareness: either can be promoted as being beneficial using evolution as a justification.

Thirdly, it is perfectly possible, again in terms of the theory of evolution, for belief in a *fictitious God* to be an adaptive advantage. We have no difficulty in talking about Father Christmas as a real person in order to make Christmas more exciting for children. In the same way, it can be argued that belief in God, even if it is not true, provides hope in the face of adversity. It could also be argued that it is an effective vehicle for the maintenance of social order when applied judiciously. Radical evolutionists should, therefore, weigh up whether the abuses carried out under the name of religion are outshone by the hope and sense of community which many religious groups experience, particularly when faced with an external threat. They should be asking which is the stronger for the species in the long term rather than which is more morally reprehensible. This kind of analysis is clearly missing from many evolutionary writers.[54]

---

[54]   Richard Dawkins' book *The God Delusion* is a telling example of this type of one-sided analysis.

So, there are difficulties in what timescale to employ in measuring evolutionary benefit: secondly, assessing the relative strength of social justice against dictatorship is problematic in terms of species fitness, and finally, encouraging false belief in some contexts could be a positive factor for an evolutionist who does not believe in God. Despite these discursive problems, a key claim of the Enlightenment was not that 'God created man' but that 'man created God', and the next section considers the rationale behind this contention.

Arguments for Atheism

Is the notion of 'God' just an adult form of 'Father Christmas'?

There are in fact more subtle arguments which lean towards atheism or at least agnosticism than the materialist one. David Hume conducts his discourse in the form of a conversation between three characters in a work called the *Dialogues*. Philo, one of the characters, as Alexander Broadie explains, "thinks the design argument a hopeless instrument for learning anything about God. His reason is that the argument relies on a supposed analogy between the natural order and human artefacts, and yet the analogy is so slight as to be vanishingly small".[55] In other words, drawing design parallels between nature and human construction is at best doubtful, so to draw a parallel between human and divine creativity is fraught with even greater difficulties. Hume asks, "Can we argue from the circulation of blood in people to the circulation of sap in trees? Surely the analogy is far too weak to permit such a conclusion".[56] It is mistaken to look for a creative design

---

[55] *The Scottish Enlightenment*, page 133
[56] Ibid, page 133

simply by identifying a common factor between various phenomena where the differences are far greater than what is in common.

Consequently, the kind of analogy between building a house and God creating the world is too weak to sustain, especially if it is coupled with a realization that human ideas are not objective accounts but fundamentally counterparts or derivatives of the sensory impressions that we experience (Hume's description of this was discussed in Chapter 1). For Hume, the idea of God is fashioned out of the need to find intelligible and consoling answers when we are confronted by fear, terror and all the pain that goes with the negative passions. Of course, this may be the case, but it does not in itself throw any light on whether God exists. Hume believed life is too complex to infer a complete explanation of everything and it is also mistaken to assume human beings are the reference point from which all intelligibility and meaning should be derived. Broadie again describes Hume's position: "The near-universality of belief in a deity points to near universal features of human nature, while at the same time carrying no implication whatever for the truth, or otherwise, of what is believed".[57] To use a frivolous example, just because laughing is a near universal trait, it does not mean that the cosmic force behind the natural world is primarily humour: Hume shows how easy it is to extrapolate the supposed character of God out of our own experience.

It is far harder, however, to see how belief in God diminishes just because knowledge of natural processes is on the increase: the latter does not directly replace the former. Nevertheless, scientific knowledge, for Hume, did replace early primitive thoughts like seeing "faces in the moon".[58] As we discover more about physical

---

[57]   Ibid, page 126
[58]   *The Scottish Enlightenment*, page 124

processes, the need to personify physical phenomena is diminished. The argument is persuasive but not conclusive because the more we discover about the material world, the greater the control we have over it and that control does lead to a stronger sense of belief, a belief in ourselves. That in itself is understandable, but with it comes a growing sense of power which belongs to an agent capable of purposive action and now one which can interfere with nature.

The Impasse

Can the ideas of 'randomness' and 'intentional creativity' mix? Is the problem more complex than it first appears to be?

We arrive at the polarity between believers in a Creator God and evolutionists who consider they need look no further than natural selection for answers. Those who **do believe** in an intelligent designer God tend to shy away from explaining why random selection is part of that creative endeavour. For evolutionists, the question of how something based on random chance can be the product of design is a pivotal issue which prevents them from believing in a creative intelligence. However, one problem with this latter view is that it implies that the whole of life must be based on chance. If I look at a tree and see it is a beautiful design, I am deceiving myself because evolution has made it look **as if it were** designed; if I paint **that tree** on a canvas and then look at it, I am entitled to say **it is** beautifully designed and crafted, of course, **by me.**

So, the key question is about the opposition between chance and design. How has intelligibility and intentionality emerged from random chemical, physical and other purely physical interactions? We do have one empirical source to examine this dilemma, at least in principle, and that is human life itself.[59] How do chance and intentionality interact? In everyday life, we are quite used to such occurrences. For example, take these two scenarios:

> I trained to be a civil engineer and by chance a friend of mine left a newspaper behind with some relevant adverts in it. Unbeknown to him, I applied for one of the positions and got the job I wanted.

> My colleague fell sick and so I had to make a business trip to Brazil; while I was there, I met my wife and thirty years later we had our first grandchild.

The point of these imaginary snapshots is to bring out how our intentions are combined with chance events: an intention to get a job coupled with the chance of a newspaper left behind, or a business trip for the company I work for with the unexpected outcome of meeting a life partner.

So why does the conjunction of randomness and divine intention seem so foreign to our sense of what is possible, given that we experience a mixture of intention and unpredictability in our daily lives? Perhaps the perceived problem with the intelligent designer theory is that it makes the original cause of life purely intentional, when we are surrounded by scientific evidence which signals a much more complex picture. We have difficulty in envisaging a possibility where an invisible mind has created our very visible physical world. How can you have a mind without a body? The echoes of grief after the loss of a loved one, the idea that Shakespeare's works are immortal, or

---

[59] The animal kingdom may of course also have something equivalent to offer in terms of the intentional behaviours that animals can exhibit.

reports of out of body experiences point us towards the possibility of alternative dimensions, but somehow they are not conclusive enough in themselves for us to firmly believe in a transcendent creator God.[60]

Nevertheless, the likelihood of a creative force behind the natural world is consistent with the beginnings of life holding the potential for a species like ours to evolve, as long as that creative force is *outside* of space and time. This is because space and time are dimensions that vary, expand and can collapse: on this account, they must be created. We are familiar with intentionality within the physical world as we know it, but it is beyond our imagination to think that such an intentionality could exist in another realm. Believing in a creative God is also to believe in that kind of mystery.

We might ask, how can a being who knows everything *create anything*? In other words, anything that is 'created' by an all-knowing being is *not new*. This question relies on the assumption that knowledge is finite, that there is a limit somewhere out there of all there is to know. That of course is an untestable assumption, even with our astonishing leaps in scientific knowledge over the last century. Human experience is based on limited knowledge which expands step by step, and not always accurately. It is very easy to imagine that the divine mind is just a bigger version of ours, but this is a mistake. Perhaps believers and opponents of transcendence both make the 'God' they are talking about into a being whose intentional attributes can be described in human terms.

If there is a God, we should only be able to understand a very small part of the divine mind. So, in talking and thinking about God,

---

[60] Many who call themselves Christians hold their faith in relation to the person of Christ rather than there being conclusive scientific evidence for the creation of the natural world. However, the belief in Christ entails belief in a non-material Creator-Father figure. My friend, Tim Edwards, adds this clarification: "That faith incorporates the idea of Christ as God incarnate. Belief in a divine Christ entails the belief in a non-material 'Father' behind him."

believers and non-believers, when they seek to criticise religion, need to bear in mind that God is much greater than our conception of Him. Dawkins, a non-believer, writes in *The Greatest Show on Earth* about giraffes in the context of how *he* would have designed the giraffe's laryngeal nerve.

> The recurrent laryngeal nerve in any mammal is good evidence against a designer. And in the giraffe it stretches from good to spectacular! That bizarrely long detour down the giraffe's neck and back up again is exactly the kind of thing we expect from evolution by natural selection, and exactly the kind of thing we do *not* expect from any kind of intelligent designer.[61]

Dawkins suggests *he would have designed* giraffes differently if God had awarded him the design contract for nature. He is equally guilty of the anthropomorphic charge brought by Spinoza and Hume against believers.

The claim from those who support the Intelligent Design theory is that God *created* the world rather than *designed* it.[62] In other words, the picture is not one of God sitting at a large table with a set of raw materials in front of Him; it is rather a picture of Him outside of space and time with nothing in front, behind, above or below him. Space and time are themselves physical entities which are not absolute. And, in any event, design does not necessarily imply determinism, as the following passage illustrates:

---

[61] *The Greatest Show on Earth, The Evidence for Evolution,* page 364

[62] This point is made using the following definitions from The Concise Oxford Dictionary (1996) Ninth Edition. BCA Oxford University Press; 'design' can be defined as a preliminary plan, sketch or concept for the making or production of a building, machine, garment etc page 366. To 'create' means "(of natural and historical forces) to bring into existence." page 315

An intelligent designer could factor in randomness because 'He' knows all possible outcomes of all possible (random) events. This is not Determinism, which says that God determines all outcomes, but absolute knowledge of all outcomes (as opposed to power over them).[63] Intelligibility could therefore be built into random natural selection without automatically dispensing with a creator-God. In this sense, intelligent design doesn't preclude randomness, nor does the latter preclude intelligibility (whether divine or human). This means a distinction has to be made between a universe that has been designed (i.e. determined – 'design' here implying omnipotence) and a universe that has had randomness designed into it (i.e. non-determined – 'design' here implying omniscience). Randomness in itself is not a sufficient argument against intelligent design.[64]

Intelligibility and Random Selection

Scientists now interfere with random selection processes and use their cognitive capacities to do so. So, before human beings arrived, it was far easier to depict the natural world as a product of accident. Now that human beings can intervene in the genetic aspects of nature, should the power of mind should be seen in a different light?

There is a more pressing problem within the dilemma between random selection and intentional creativity than simply identifying false attributions to God. Once a species is capable of manipulating

---

[63] Or power which is not exercised.
[64] This comment was added by my friend Tim Edwards to assist in clarifying the point.

genetic structures, it is effectively placing a limit on the power of the evolutionary process.

Not only has scientific knowledge led to the possibility of genetically modified designer babies, human activity has interrupted the evolutionary flow.[65] In 2016, Dr Vallejo-Marin described the research into a plant known as the Shetlands Monkeyflower. She explained how the transporting of animal and plant species to new habitats could lead to new species: what took thousands or millions of years without human intervention could now take place in a couple of hundred.[66]

Natural selection is not necessarily the sole and dominant force in nature. It is not unassailable and *can* be changed through human migration, intelligent research and *redesign*. The whole picture is far more complex than simply attaching 'evolution' as a tag line to every psychological, social and philosophical theory. Were random selection to be the overriding influence in the natural world, intelligibility would be at best mistaken and at worst a delusion. Why is it possible to make coherent sense of the notion of a random force? Describing a phenomenon as random, chaotic and unpredictable is, paradoxically, to give those very qualities a conceptual framework. More crucially, science itself cannot operate without intelligibility.[67]

As Domasio explains, Spinoza's gentle attempt to "tear the mask of human personality from the idea of God" to "join forces ... in the possibilities of science" was aimed to maintain a sense of reverence

---

[65] In July 2018, The Nuffield Council on Bioethics said changing the DNA of a human embryo could be 'morally permissible' if it is in the child's best interests.

[66] For more on this study go to *https://www.shetlandtimes.co.uk/2017/08/16/isles-monkey-flower-new-species*

[67] This has been vigorously debated by Professor John Lennox and Professor Richard Dawkins.

for nature whilst dispensing with the personhood of God.[68] There is still an attraction for many to use traditional theology with modern atheistic rationalism. It fashions a sense of inclusion for those with a scientific outlook and suggests a generosity of spirit towards tradition and those who hold their faith dear. However, there is a crucial, if mysterious, interplay between firstly, our capacity for abstract thought and imagination about the physical world, and secondly, the impersonal processes which are woven into it.

We should, however, examine the possible implications of our own ability to manipulate some aspects of natural selection through intelligibility itself. Intelligent *redesign* of our genetic functioning, at least in part, is achievable by us, and genetic 'creativity' is also becoming possible. To sustain the atheistic evolutionary position, it now becomes necessary to claim that humans *are* capable of *intelligent design*, but *only humans*. It is a fantastic mystery that the natural world is both a product of random selection and is also intelligible. The fact that it is a mystery should immediately tell us that it is mistaken to try and trace God's finger as intervention in every quirk of nature or claim the opposite, that we are little more than the result of chance genetic interactions with the environment. To contradict the atheist position does not of itself carry with it any accompanying assertion about the existence of a Creator God. For the agnostic, it is not a matter of leaping from the existence of intelligibility to the existence of a creator God: that is a separate issue, but nevertheless the relation between science and the intelligibility required for its practice is a factor which should be included in any consideration of that wider transcendent issue.

---

[68] *Looking For Spinoza, Joy, Sorrow and the Feeling Brain*, page 96. Spinoza thought that we could train our minds to master the passions; he did not conceive that we might visit and amend the inner workings of their genetic structure.

Concluding Remark

> Evolution has to account for intelligent design by human beings. It may be worth asking how far the human capacity for rational thought can take us. This is the subject of the next chapter.

In summary, the atheistic evolutionist's most acute criticism of intelligent design is based on the disparity between the haphazard way the natural world has developed and the sense of order which accounts such as Genesis, even if they are symbolic, convey. The proponents of intelligent design, on the other hand, say that atheistic evolutionists struggle to integrate the power of mind into their theory, especially given its potential power to intervene in natural processes.

So how can the discussion be taken forward, particularly for those who do not feel secure in either camp? One way is to examine what the limits, if any, of rational enquiry are.[69] This means exploring whether our rationality can fathom all aspects of human nature and functionality. For rationality to be seen as the arbiter of all issues, it also has to address the more complicated and inaccessible parts of human morality and unconscious life. Such a discussion may not lead to any kind of precise answer, but it may provide a better position to ask whether humans are suitably qualified to be masters of their own destiny.

---

[69] The word 'rational' is being introduced here because it allows for a more detailed philosophical enquiry into the human capacity to think. Reasoning is a close associate of 'rationality', discussed in Chapter 9. It may be helpful to think of rationality as an internal coherence which applies to intention or action, whilst reasoning refers to the comparison between different explanations. However, as you will see, there are varying ways in which the word 'rationality' is used.

Chapter 4
Rationality – Our Best Hope?

We have asserted ourselves over nature by using our rational powers. What does rationality mean? Is it just a technique for thinking, or is it a belief that we can solve any problem through reason?

The last chapter ended by posing the question as to whether our capacity for 'rational' thinking might be strong enough for us to be masters of our own destiny, thereby excluding the need for an external transcendent God. The discussion has so far focussed on our human potential to master the forces in nature, but this necessarily involves how such mastery over nature should be used. In short, is rationality capable of controlling the self-destructive tendencies of the human species? There is no single answer to this question, but an examination of how the concept of 'rationality' works will shed light on it. The discussion in this chapter will also lay the ground for the following chapter where the idea of 'rationality' is applied to evolution, to a combination of evolution and creation, and finally to creationist theology.

At the very outset of this chapter, it is important to note that the meaning of 'rationality' is contested by philosophers. Some philosophers focus on what it is in human beings which marks them out from the higher animals, some are intent on uncovering a universal formula for 'rationality' which can be applied in any context and some apply the word with an associated moral undertone. In examining these three approaches to rationality, their respective strengths and shortfalls will become apparent. It is at once obvious that each interpretation carries with it an implication: the first focuses on finding a *difference* between us and animals, the second on *divesting* the term from any particular application of it and the third in *prescribing* the outcome to be achieved through its correct use. 'Rationality' is, therefore, a contested concept because it can be used for differing purposes.

The term 'rationality' is used in a whole variety of contexts. When challenged by a difficult situation at work I might think later on, 'I could have dealt with it more rationally'. When listening to a politician, the term 'most rational solution' might be used: or a scientist reviewing a research brief may consider a particular line of research to be the 'most rational one' to pursue.

The philosopher Alasdair Macintyre, writing about 'justice', claims that an exploration into the concept of 'rationality' is needed before any substantive enquiry. He says, "To know what justice is, so it may seem, we must first learn what rationality in practice requires of us".[70] What he means by this is what 'rational' is for the individual may not be 'rational' for the group as a whole. So, it might be 'rational' for me to gain as much wealth as possible, but it might not be 'rational' for the whole of society to have a few very rich people and a lot of malnourished people. The implications for the study of 'justice' are apparent. Furthermore, he suggests that the "ultimate and true good of human beings" may contradict the first two notions: for example, some may believe that the whole of society should return to a simpler, less materialistic life style.[71] For this, a different sense of 'rationality'

---

[70]   *Whose Justice? Which Rationality?* page 2
[71]   Ibid, page 2

would apply. How we use the concept of 'rationality' is shaped by what we want to achieve. The next section examines the notion of 'rationality' which separates us from the higher animals.

A Unique Characteristic

Rationality is the ability to reason above and beyond one's immediate environment – is this trait uniquely human?

What is it that marks us out from animals who can signal to each other, work together to avert danger and divide up tasks and roles without deliberation? Rational creatures, to use Jonathan Bennett's 1964 model, can think about managing their environment without having to be *in it*. The following passage demonstrates what he is trying to get at:

Suppose that a highly intelligent sheepdog showed itself able to understand a really complex system of whistles by the shepherd, and also showed itself to be master of a complex system of barking noises from which the shepherd could infer much useful information about the position of the sheep, the nature of the terrain and so on. This begins to sound like the story about a genuine, if primitive, language. But [sic] suppose it transpired that the dog would bark 'informatively' even when the shepherd was out of earshot; suppose it never passed on the informative barks of another similarly endowed dog; suppose it never learned that (say) when the shepherd removed his hat his whistles were always lies … in these ways the dog showed itself to be entirely unadaptable and thus unintelligent about many other things.[72]

The dog shows intelligence through his understanding of the whistles: it shows capacity to understand a signal. The dog is unable, however, to extend his intelligences to the extent of being able to work *without* the shepherd. For that he would need Bennett's version of rationality, the ability to fit the shepherd's past actions (a dated judgement) into the scheme of the shepherd's overall aim for the sheep (a universal judgement). If the dog were capable of this, he would then be in a position to *decide* if he wanted to go along with the shepherd's aims or not: to do that he would have to be able to think in abstract terms by connecting what the shepherd did with what the shepherd wants. Bennett maintains that this is not the reality and so there is a huge gulf between the competence of dogs and humans: 'rationality', he says, is the suitable word to describe the missing element. The dog, as far as we know, is not sitting in his kennel wondering what will happen to him when the shepherd retires.

Take, for example, the need which human beings have to avoid exposure to the cold. In a primitive society, the children of that society might die in large numbers because they do not have adequate protection. I discover that I feel warmer when I have an animal skin wrapped around me. I try wrapping a skin round my child and discover she survives when others who do not have that protection die. I could, of course, make the wrong association, perhaps thinking that the animal skin has magic powers. However, I eventually realise that when she is wearing the skin she is warmer, and the children who have died have all been very cold to touch. So, I decide that

---

[72] *Rationality, An Essay towards Analysis*, page 47

the particular instance of my child keeping warm through wearing the animal skin means that **all** the children should wear them.[73] I make a universal judgement based on a particular event. In order to do that I have to make two connections: firstly, between the use of the skin and the resulting warmth felt by my child and secondly, applying that discovery to all the children in my community. This second connection requires a 'what if' abstract idea and it is that which Bennett considers to be the kernel of 'rationality'.[74] I try and persuade another member of my group that using animal skins to keep children warm is a good idea and therefore we should provide them for all. 'Rationality', on this account, becomes a shared tool in a social context: theoretically it could work on its own if the ability to think could *fully* emerge without appropriate nurture. However, the experience of finding feral and abused children who have been kept in near total isolation shows this is not possible.

If this is an acceptable account of how 'rationality' works, then it can be argued that 'rationality' separates us from animals like the sheepdog. However, the story does not stop here. Once basic needs are met, questions arise as to how many animals to kill in order to clothe ourselves, how many clothes each person needs and which is the most humane process through which to make those clothes. Furthermore, how should the process of making clothes be organised, who should do it, and should there be particular rewards for particular tasks? What happens when we are in a position to choose between how many clothes we need and how many we want?

---

[73] The question of why I might want all the children to be kept warm cannot be averted, but the point here is that I have the ability to make the connection between a single instance and a potential universal application of it.

[74] Whereas the first connection could be justified by association (using the behaviourist model of learning), the second is much harder to justify in those terms because, to put it simply, it requires a leap of imagination.

In other words, the mastery over the environment which this form of 'rationality' provides also throws up an array of other dilemmas about the sustainability of the animal population, roles, rewards and status. When does fashion enter the equation? The 'rationality' needed to make a product carries with it many moral and political questions for the group in question. These must be addressed if the manufacture of clothes is to continue without disruption.

It seems an integral part of representing 'rationality' in the way I have so far, is to be able to use experience to formulate abstract possibilities, some of which can then be tested out in reality. This is the way Bennett and Macintyre frame it and Ian Jarvie, philosopher and anthropologist, also does. Jarvie says that science is the paradigm of "learning from experience" because it shows how we accumulate knowledge, building on what we already know through very broad methods of "trial and error".[75] Jarvie, whose background is in anthropology, distinguishes between rationality which is **goal orientated** and that which is **predictable**.[76] Rain dances can be rational because they are based on "**some** body of ideas and information" but not the "**best** standard"[77] (emphasis added). Science for Jarvie is the strongest type of 'rationality' because it uses predictability as a measure of success.

This model of 'rationality' is a 'cognitive toolkit' for mastery over the environment, either directly or through other people. However, there is an altogether different model based on the notion of self-contradiction: this reductionist model seeks to find a formula for 'rationality' that can apply to anything at all because it does not examine the nature of the content; rather, it looks at the internal

---

75   *Rationality and Relativism, In search of a philosophy and history of anthropology,*
      page 52
76   He refers to these as weak and strong forms of rationality (48).
77   Ibid pages 48-49

coherence of intentions. It is represented by the Oxford philosopher, John Broome.

Internal Coherence

> What happens when we narrow down the meaning of rationality to simply ensure that the connection between our intentions and beliefs makes sense?

Professor John Broome's account of rationality involves linking our **intentions** with what we believe we **ought** to do. The kind of 'ought' he is referring to depends on human agency rather than its more general use such as 'it ought to be sunnier than this', which is another way of saying 'I would like it to be sunny'. This is not relevant to Broome's discussion as to what constitutes 'rationality'.

Broome says, "We can say that rationality requires people to intend to do what they ought to do".[78] This initially appears to be a very limited account of what many understand rationality to entail. It appears straightforward if what we think we ought to do is uncontroversial, for example going to work. If we think we ought to go to work it is clearly 'rational' to intend to walk to the bus stop at the relevant time to travel there; our **intention** to catch the bus is clearly linked to our belief that we **ought** to get to work on time.

However, the issue becomes far more opaque when we are faced by conflicting influences. If I believe that I should tell my parents the truth about the vase I broke but am frightened of their reaction, I may decide to deceive them and suggest it was the cat's fault. It could of course be argued that I actually decided I **ought not** to

---

[78] *Rationality Through Reasoning*, page 2

face their wrath and therefore my *intention* to deceive was rational. Strictly speaking, this may be true in the context of that moment, but it ignores the conflict between what I would normally consider obligatory, i.e. to tell the truth, and what I did on this occasion. I could have decided to tell my parents the truth, that I did knock the vase over, and that would have been *equally* 'rational'. So 'rationality', on this account, does *not* inform me which course to take.

Defining rationality in such narrow terms does nothing to resolve anything wider than the coherence of a particular action by a particular individual at a particular time. Broome is quite clear about this: "Enkrasia [the technical term for this version of 'rationality'] is a matter of internal coherence among your mental attitudes; it is not a matter of the relation between those attitudes and the world".[79] Macintyre puts it in a different way: "So it has sometimes been claimed ... that there can be no uniquely rational way of ordering goods within a scheme of life, but rather that there are numerous alternative modes of ordering, in the choice between which there are no sufficient good reasons to guide us".[80] 'Rationality' in this model cannot tell us what the overall solution to the problem at hand is, it can only present a number of possible alternatives.

If my parents suspect that I am not telling them the truth, their *intention* to question me because they think they *ought* to be told the truth is also rational for them. That particular 'ought' does not dovetail with my intention *not* to tell my parents that I broke the vase. 'Oughts' can conflict with each other, but for Broome only *between* people. 'Rationality' comes into play once I have made *my* mind up

[79] *Rationality Through Reasoning*, page 174
[80] *Whose Justice? Which Rationality?* page 133

what to do.[81] Even if Broome's account strictly applies to individual actions, it depends on the individual always being *single minded* and never caught in the middle of two conflicting 'oughts', in this case whether or not I should tell my parents the truth about the vase. Certainly what is rational from my parents' view about the vase may not be favoured by me, and deciding what is rational for the family as a whole seems beyond the scope of Broome's definition. If the issue is about minimising distress, albeit by taking the risk of lying, then a different 'ought' is involved to the one that applies should the prime concern be about the overall trust between my parents and me in the longer term. Broome's definition of rationality and any variants of it cannot help in deciding which of those issues should be given priority. Where the idea of internal coherence carries greater weight is where a single theory is used as a foundation for everything: as already mentioned, this will be examined in relation to evolution, creationism and a mixture of creation and evolution in Chapter 5.

Broome does not claim that we human beings are fully 'rational'; his main concern is to arrive at a strict definition of what rationality entails. That approach to defining 'rationality' is, however, totally insufficient for those who believe that the combination of reason, information and evidence can be used as the main method to find solutions to social, political and scientific questions. Once the focal

---

[81] Many studies of individual differences in reasoning focus on individual functioning. Keith Stanovitch in *Who is Rational? Studies of Individual Differences in Reasoning*, for example, implies those of higher intelligence are more likely to rationalise in a way that maximises personal benefit, but those of lower ability may instead act in a way that better promotes evolutionary adaptation. "When interpreting these outcomes, it helps to distinguish between evolutionary adaptation and instrumental rationality (utility maximization given goals and beliefs).The key point for the latter (variously termed practical, pragmatic, or means/ends rationality) maximization is at the level of the individual person" (page 148). Such studies cannot directly inform the debate as to what our social and political priorities should be.

point of rationality moves from intention to outcome, the issue of which outcome is the most important necessarily imports a value judgement into the equation. Consequently, a more problematic question arises: how can rationality help in deciding what our social and political priorities should be? The next section considers whether Broome's internal coherence and Jarvie's test of predictability are sufficient tools to solve the problems caused by bad science and the misguided use of faith.

Applying 'Rationality'

What happens when we try to apply theories of 'rationality' to real situations?

Consider these two scenarios, the Thalidomide scandal of the 1960s and the Wesley Barker tragedy in 1978. Firstly, the Thalidomide scandal: in the 1950s a West German pharmaceutical company produced an anticonvulsive drug which was not tested on pregnant animals before release. Thalidomide, as it became known, was sold over the counter and was found to reduce morning sickness in pregnancy. It led to the birth of over 10,000 disabled children. It led to more rigorous testing for new drugs in the U.S. and the U.K. It was, however found to alleviate symptoms of leprosy and there are still concerns about its black-market use, particularly in developing countries, carrying with it the risk of more disabled children being born.

Secondly, in 1978 Wesley Barker's parents took him to a faith healer and then disposed of his insulin, believing their faith could heal him. His father believed the diabetes was caused by demons.

Even after the boy died, the father still believed the boy would be brought back to life and refused to believe otherwise (from Jarvie).[82]

In terms of learning from those situations *now*, a proper assessment would involve knowing what impact the Thalidomide story had on future drug trialling and what impact Wesley Barker's story had on other parents considering withdrawing medical care for their children for faith-based reasons. In practice, the impact assessment for both situations is fraught with methodological difficulties. Finding all the parents who had been affected by the Wesley Barker story might be difficult, and even if found, their accounts may be biased through the additional pressure placed on participants by the presence of the researcher. The story of Thalidomide shows that the 1960s episode did not prevent its use in Africa and other developing countries in more recent times. So, evaluating *the extent* of purely '*rational adjustments*' made in consequence is problematic.

We can, however, speculate and ask what a 'rational' response to the scenarios would look like. In relation to the Thalidomide scandal, most people would consider it appropriate to invoke more rigorous testing before drugs are made clinically available, and for companies to regulate who they sell the drugs to. What becomes clearer in looking at this example is that *something more* than 'learning from experience' is being appealed to. Underlying such an outcome is the ethical value of respecting life and using all available means to support that value. Marcus Aurelius, an ancient writer, suggested that rationality could only flourish provided we do not give our selfish inclinations free reign. He wrote, "It is not right that the rational and social good should be rivalled by anything of a different order, for example the praise of the many, or power, or wealth, or the enjoyment

---

of pleasure".[83] In other words, learning more about the aetiology of an illness is the 'rational' component, but directing that knowledge for the good of others is about a different type of intent, namely the promotion of wellbeing.

For the tragic story of Wesley Barker, it is reasonable to suggest the parents were simply deluded and their thinking was irrational. Whilst I agree with this wholeheartedly, I still want to explore the situation further. Whereas the body produces both insulin and water naturally, we still need to drink water to keep us healthy. The very same applies to insulin: some people like Wesley Barker need to take insulin to regulate the sugar levels in their blood. Presumably his parents did not deny him water; on that basis, neither should they have denied him insulin. It is, in this context, absurd to say the diabetes was a result of demon possession. However, the parents' unshakeable belief was to do with their own interpretation of the situation in religious terms. They could neither think of or accept a 'rational' alternative from within the foundations of their own faith. For instance, they could have been encouraged to think that God would want them to care for their son in whatever way possible and their faith should be directed to ask God to watch over the situation *whatever* happened. It was not for them to 'instruct' God. To accept this would mean that they would not have been playing 'Russian Roulette' with their son's life but would still have been maintaining their faith. Whereas they might have felt this to be a weaker stance, their own position rested on the implicit assumption that they had to *prove* the strength of their faith for other people to see. There is no such requirement in theological terms, so the 'rational' alternative suggested is a credible one. Strangely enough, Broome's internal coherence theory is applicable here because it implies that there are

---

[83]   *Meditations*, page 27

'rational' **alternatives**. If there are 'rational' alternatives in relation to anything it means that we do not have the **whole story** (as we will see later on). If Wesley Barker's parents had thought about their situation in similar vein, both medically and existentially, he may have survived.[84]

It was the self-assessment of how much both the doctors and the parents themselves knew in relation to what they did **not know** which was critical: the doctors did not exhaust all the 'rational' alternatives when testing the drug, and the parents did not explore the 'rational' faith alternatives in relation to their son. So, Broome's model expresses 'rationality' as a tool which can open up various alternatives, whilst Jarvie's 'learning from experience' model requires something more than knowledge if the outcomes are to benefit other people.

One of the main themes in this book is whether science and faith can coexist without compromising each other. There are two core issues: firstly, what is the connection between these two distinct forms of knowledge, and secondly, how those forms of knowledge are used. In this latter sense, the idea of using 'rational' capacities for the good of others comes into play.

Rationality as Respect

> We can employ internal consistency in our thinking, we can learn how the physical world works but what should we do with that knowledge?

Immanuel Kant, the eighteenth century philosopher closely associated with the Enlightenment, speaks of rationality being misused. He

---

[84] Any human situation is more complex than isolating one or two factors, but I am using this tragic event to illustrate the nature and limits of rationality.

says, when describing anyone who has not learnt to think for himself: "Dogmas and formulas, those mechanical instruments for *rational* use (or rather misuse) of his natural endowments, are the ball and chain of his permanent immaturity."[85]

Rationality can be mistaken, as it was in the Thalidomide case, but more than that, Kant here is saying it can be used slavishly in the pursuit of dogma, as Wesley Barker's parents did. They claimed the truth had been set down by a higher authority and then used interpretations (which were 'rational' insofar as they were internally consistent) to justify those immovable principles. The Dutch Reformed church used (or as Kant and many others would say, 'misused') Biblical passages about separating peoples into different languages to justify Apartheid. In other words, their position was coherent even though it is now morally repellent to the modern western democratic mind. For Kant, this kind of justification is based on dogma; it is not so much irrational, but the *misuse* of rationality.

A modern comparison might be made between the western democratic value of tolerance and the perceived mentality of terrorists who believe their acts of violence, often symbolically sealed with suicide, are justified as acts of judgement on Western decadence. The terrorist is not being irrational, according to Kantian rationality, but grossly misusing the gift of being able to form a reasoned argument. *Believing* in a rationale or an ideology relies on actions being driven by the conscious rather than the unconscious mind. As such, the stated intentions are 'rational' even though they are cemented into a foundation which prohibits the exploration of alternatives. 'Rationality' which censors freedom of thought can only be a distorted version of it. A broader context in which rationality should be framed has already been referred to in the writings of

---

[85]   *The Answer to the Question: What is Enlightenment?* page 2

Marcus Aurelius; it includes the moral and social dimensions of rational thought and action. Kant concurs with Aurelius' approach:

> There is more chance of an entire public enlightening ... if only the public concerned is left in freedom. For there will always be a few who think for themselves, even among those appointed as guardians of the common mass. Such guarantees, once they have themselves thrown off the yoke of immaturity, will disseminate the spirit of **rational** respect for personal value and for the duty of all men to think for themselves.[86]

Jarvie claims science to be the purest form of 'rationality' because it involves building on what is already known to the point of having predictive power. He distinguishes science from scientific activity which is pitted with the flaws of any human activity. The question then arises as to whether the progress in understanding the natural world and the mechanics of space and time has been matched by a similar increase in **the rational respect for others**.

In other words, Kant's "rational respect" refers to the substance of human interaction.[87] This of course is much harder to assess in terms of linear progress. The point, however, is that this type of rationality is about how human beings should behave towards one another, using the idea that it is rational to treat others in the way one would expect to be treated oneself. Kant's perspective, known as The Categorical Imperative, is based on the assumption that humans recognise themselves as **fully** rational beings and therefore "act only according to that maxim whereby you can at the same time will that

---

[86]   *The Answer to the Question: What is Enlightenment?* pages 2-3
[87]   Ibid, page 3

it should become a universal law".[88] The question arises as to whether it is realistic to devise a moral law on the assumption that rationality outweighs other influences to the point that elements of poverty, upbringing, and susceptibility to isolation, depression and abuse can be subjugated.

What really motivates us to respect others? Is reason the prime motivator or is it just part of our repertoire of instincts, nurturing experience, and cultural inheritance? Is it going too far to say, as Hume did, that reason is "slave of the passions"? [89] Broome, a champion of the limiting case for rationality, is also clear that "none of us satisfies all the requirements of rationality, so none of us is fully rational".[90] There is no clear-cut answer and, so as far as rationality being able to help us become masters of our own destiny is concerned, the best we can say is that the jury is out. If factors ranging from internal coherence, prediction, learning from experience and respect for others are all constituents of 'rationality', then what does it actually mean? It may be that it is impossible to arrive at a narrowed down definition: each element could reflect a particular cultural aspiration.

Nevertheless, if we want to continue to try and define 'rationality', we have to return to the issue of what **counts as knowledge**. If knowledge covers our cognitive and social experience as well as being related to our deeper feelings, rational enquiry should address the whole range even if it means being honest about those things we 'know' but cannot articulate. In our quest to fathom out our significance, all parts of our lives should ideally be **integrated with each other**.

---

88 *Kant, A complete introduction*, page 154
89 *A Treatise of Human Nature*, page 462
90 *Rationality Through Reasoning*, page 155

Imagine you are interested in learning Mandarin, ballet dancing and writing poetry. You have some understanding of all three, but over a very recent period of six months you appear to have made remarkable progress in your ballet technique. You decide that learning Mandarin and writing poetry should both be based on ballet dancing techniques; when you announce this you are met, unsurprisingly, with incredulity.

Now imagine that over the last four thousand years we have pursued scientific knowledge, sought to enjoy relationships and family life and develop our ability to paint and sculpt. In the last two hundred years, there has been a sudden acceleration in our scientific knowledge. We decide to base our family relationships and our artistic activities on the principles we have used to develop our scientific knowledge. Although that decision can be justified as 'rational', the question arises as to whether such a strategy is the best way to **integrate** the various types of knowledge and experiences we enjoy.

Chapter 5
'Rationality' – How does it apply to Evolution, Intentionality and Creationist Theology?

In this chapter, the idea of rationality is applied to evolution, creative intentionality and a combination of the two.

In the previous chapter, I argued that it is impossible to isolate 'rationality' from the context of life in which it is being used. In preparation for a re-evaluation of evolution and faith in a creator, I want to apply the notion of rationality to three standpoints: evolution *without* creation, evolution *as part of* creation, and finally to creationist theology, which is creation *without* evolution.

Rationality: a matter of intent or perception?

Can big ideas like evolution, belief in a Creator, or creationism sometimes contain factors which do not fit in with the main thrust of that viewpoint?

In the last chapter, 'rationality' was described in different ways: as a form of internal coherence, the means through which we test theories to improve our knowledge of the world, and lastly as the motivation for promoting the good of others. They all hold a connection between the intention and the intended outcome, so these versions of 'rationality' all depend on someone being behind the intention. To ask, then, whether a particular theory is 'rational' is really to ask two things: does it make sense with itself and what is its scope? How much can a theory explain? This use of 'rationality' is not so much a question of intention as of perception: what light does it shed on **the way we see** the world? The way we interpret our lives and the world around us is relevant to our intentions, although the connection may not always be immediate. However, the symmetry between our view of how the world should be and our actions is not always straightforward.

Consider the following example: I believe that it is wrong to murder someone (which I do!) and I then become overcome with rage and commit murder. Was my act an irrational act? Even though I have a belief that committing murder is wrong, I did have an intention to murder and carried it out. I knew what I was doing, and my intention led to the act, so using the enkratic definition, my act was rational.[91] So a rational act can contradict a belief system which opposes such acts. It's clear that murder as a way of life is detrimental to any species that relies on a degree of social solidarity for its survival. It is, therefore, 'rational' that murder is wrong for society. The respective 'rationalities' of individual acts of murder contradict the 'rationality' which supports evolutionary fitness.

---

[91] Enkratic reasoning is where a belief leads to an intention. Enkratic rationality is where I act in a way which I think I ought to act. In the above example, I did not **reason** my way from a belief against murder to a belief in favour of it under certain conditions and then commit the specific act in this particular circumstance. The rage and anger I experienced made me think I ought to murder the person. The adjective 'enkratic' is a Greek word but the corresponding noun 'enkrateia' implies mastery over temptation. Broome's invented word 'enkrasia' carries no such connotation. This is because he is seeking to explore the basis of 'rationality' alone.

In the same way that there can be contradictions between what we believe and what we do the way we understand theories can also be problematic when we come up against factors which do not automatically fit into them.

Evolution without Creation – Physicality is the Springboard of Life

What are the implications of believing that the fundamental springboard of life is physical?

To believe that the origins of life are *purely physical* means that we *cannot also* believe that there was *intentionality* behind the origins of life. If, however, the basis of life is physical then it is perfectly 'rational' to believe that our cognitive capacity is derived from that physical basis. Rationality, in this context, is about working out the derivatives from the physical to the cognitive. It may be hard to justify in certain areas but as long as it is potentially coherent, it remains 'rational'. Kim Sterelny, uses a physical model as a blueprint for the way human cognition works. For example, he says this:

> The distinctive feature of meme theories of cultural evolution is that the replication rate of the meme, and hence its evolutionary success, is not intrinsically connected to the biological fitness of the meme's bearer.[92]

Meme theory is where certain cultural ideas have a virtual life of their own but influence the way we think and act, the most successful

---

[92] *Thought in a Hostile World; The Evolution; The Evolution of Human Cognition,* page 239

ideas gaining the most evolutionary advantage. Against this view, if the power of cognition could in principle overpower the **entire** force of evolutionary assumptions, the origins of life could not be safely said to be both random and physical. Sterenly's floating memes would not have immunity against human decision making. To do that would entail a degree of self-contradiction, to the extent that such a view would be self-contradictory the accusation of 'irrationality' could also be levied.

Creation with Evolution

> Does an evolutionary perspective which includes the seeds of cooperation in the earliest and simplest form of life leave open the question of whether there is a creative intelligence behind life?

In Chapter 2, I referred to Antonio Domasio's work describing some qualities of a single bacterium which could potentially be relevant in social settings. Domasio is an evolutionist and it would be completely wrong to suggest that he has any pretensions towards creationism of any sort. Despite this, to believe that the seeds of cooperation were **inherent in the origins of life** means we can **either** believe that life is totally internally driven or that such potential is a reflection of a creative intentionality outside of space and time.

Take the following quote and decide which of these two above options was favoured by the writer.

Different proteins can self-assemble, often without any outside help, to form complex ensembles like 'biological microchips' that carry out the functions of life ... It's as if we were watching a bunch of Lego pieces in a bath and they suddenly self-assembled to form a little boat.[93]

The writer, Dennis Alexander, is a Christian. The **scientific** knowledge gaps are identical for both the evolutionist (without creation) and the believer in creation (with evolution): they are gaps, for example, in the ladder of cognitive abilities, the rise of language and the beginnings of life itself. The idea of the 'rollercoaster' of evolution can apply to both materialist and creative intelligence options when attempting to explain the cause of life, and so cannot be used by one to exclude the other.

For the believer in creation (with evolution) the idea of creating something that has its own creative force is not irrational. Why is this so? Take any great work of art, perhaps one created hundreds of years ago. As a modern-day student sees this piece of inert inorganic matter, it sparks them into creating their own 'masterpiece'. The original artist's work was creative and the student's work, triggered by the original piece, is also creative.

More pragmatically, we might think about the future and imagine we have reached a position where we possess the key ingredients to bring about the beginnings of life. The knowledge would be there to kickstart a chemical and electrical process eventually leading to organic life. It is not, therefore, irrational to believe that it is possible to create something that has a creative force of its own: humans are creative both reproductively and in other ways. If it is hypothetically possible to envisage this, it is not irrational to then believe this may have already been done, by a Creator.

---

[93]   *Creation or Evolution, Do We Have to Choose?* Page 341

Something from Nothing

Is understanding how matter existed outside of time, before the universe began, a problem?

Evolutionary theories have claimed there is no God because evolution itself has revealed biological processes which replace the notion of intentional design. For evolutionists like Dennett, once you have discovered the process you need look no further to elicit the cause, certainly in the context of the origins of life.

> *The Blind Watchmaker* (1986), [sic] nicely evokes the apparently paradoxical nature of these processes: on the one hand they are blind, mindless without goals, and on the other hand they produce designed entities galore, many of which become competent artificers (nest-builders, web-spinners, and so forth) and a few become intelligent designers and builders; us.[94]

Evolutionists potentially have a contradictory problem in that materialism denies the existence of anything transcendent, so if time had a beginning, as Stephen Hawking maintained, matter would **have had to pre-exist** in some form or other. Whether this is compatible with Einstein's theory of relativity would be a matter for physicists to pronounce on. If they were to pronounce that this is an impossibility, materialist evolutionists would face the difficulty of explaining where matter came from in the first place. It is as if another theory beyond quantum mechanics is missing. Evolutionists have to explain how a Planck size universe measuring a billion trillion trillionth of

---

[94] *From Bacteria to Bach and Back,* page 37

a centimetre was there 'before' time began. Unless they plump for Roger Penrose's theory that the universe is part of an endless cycle of expansion and contraction, this means that there is some kind of matter or energy in all worlds and self-generating factors arise under certain conditions.[95]

Theists on the other hand have no human equivalent to draw upon in explaining how something can stem from nothing. They can argue that creativity does exist in a human context, but it would require a mixture of artistic imagination and the biological engineering which modern genetics has introduced for any kind of divine creative energy to make sense. This would still not explain how matter has arisen from nothing, if indeed it has, and so they are not exempted from scientific exploration. Those who have a belief in a Creator God proffer an explanation of the intention but not of the process of how the world and life have come into being, even if it has from some kind of eternal physicality: some might even suggest that to know the whole process would amount to equality with the divine mind.

As far as the origins of life are concerned, we cannot say that information about creative intentionality is irrelevant **unless** we presuppose that the beginnings of life were purely physical. However, one cannot validate an argument by presupposing the outcome. Consequently, the **unknowns** when it comes to the beginnings of life are not automatically confined to physical dimensions alone. The gaps in our knowledge are perhaps larger in the realms where

---

[95]   There is now speculative interest in whether the dense mass at the 'beginning' of the universe was in fact not so much a Big Bang as a 'big bounce', the initial expansion following on from the 'crunch' of a previous universe contracting into a black hole, out of which our universe emerged (Thanks to Tim Edwards for pointing this out). Also see Roger Penrose's *Cycles of Time: An Extraordinary New View of the Universe* discussing the issues at stake.

we have not worked out, and perhaps cannot work out, a way of experimentally testing theories.

Creation Science without Evolution

Creation Science is based on finding a match between the Genesis account and research findings. It is criticised by evolutionists as prejudging the outcomes of scientific enquiry but evolutionists (without creation) also assume that the undiscovered aspects of the world will fit into their general theory of evolution. Have both theories something in common?

To believe the account of Creation in Genesis Chapter One, which is based on our calendar year system, means you cannot *also believe* in the timescale of evolution. The difficulty lies in explaining away the dating of rocks and fossils available through modern scientific work, the denial of which leads to ridicule from much of the scientific and modern enlightenment community. It would be 'irrational' to do both, i.e. accept the evolutionary timescale and the creationist timescale simultaneously. However, it is not 'irrational' to argue that the natural world is the result of creation, even if evolutionists believe it to be mistaken. Take the following extract from *The Creation Science Journal* about the navigational capacities of insects:

One wonders how many millions of years it took these insect groups to evolve these complex mechanisms, and how they managed to avoid getting lost and perishing in unsuitable areas in the meantime? Perhaps they were designed with these capabilities from the outset. This logical[96] alternative is completely absent from the report's discussion.[97]

What evolutionists find difficult is the suggestion that unexplained capabilities should be explained by reference to design rather than to yet unspecified processes. "Perhaps they were designed" is speculation.[98] Evolutionists, however, also speculate about undiscovered phenomena. Take this sentence from Daniel Dennett:

> The evolutionary origin of language is an unsolved, but not insoluble, problem, and both experimental and theoretical work has made progress in formulating testable hypotheses about gradual, incremental evolutionary processes, both cultural and genetic, that could transform the more primitive talents of our ancestors into the verbal dexterity and prolixity of modern language users.[99]

Despite the origins of language being unsolved, the presumption is that the solution will be found within evolutionary theory. Evolutionists object to solutions which do not fit into the overall scheme of evolutionary theory. In the example from *The Creation Science Journal*, the presumption was that unsolved problems could be explained in terms of design. It seems that regardless of any judgements about the quality of scientific work from either camp,

---

[96] The word 'reasonable' can be substituted if the objection that this inference is not a matter of strict logic is raised. In other words, the writer is conveying that there is more than one possible explanation.
[97] *Creation Science Movement Journal,* Vol 19 (Feb 2017), page 6 (D. Cockcroft)
[98] Ibid, page 6
[99] *From Bacteria to Bach and Back,* page 281

the logical structure of the objections is very similar: if there is a gap, the solution will be found within the preselected theory.

Prejudging the Unknowns

> How do we take into account what we do not know now but might know in the future?

If we are always to imagine the gaps in our knowledge as being filled by a yet unknown extension of the theory we favour, we may be guilty of an unforgiveable scientific sin, not having an open mind. This tendency must limit the range of possibilities which can be taken into account when researching unsolved problems.

Having already said that the believer in creation (with evolution) faces the same *scientific* problems faced by the evolutionist (without creation), it is worth looking at how the gaps are viewed. Believing in a creator God does not answer *any* scientific questions. What it should do, however, is leave open the possibilities of finding new theories of how the world and we ourselves work. The evolutionist (without creation) is more firmly tied to one particular scientific theory, that is, evolution. To release the theory into a competitive arena with as yet other undiscovered scientific ideas would weaken its semantic associations with the notions of 'objectivity' and 'neutrality'.

It is rational to speculate about unknowns. To speculate on possible future knowledge currently outside our understanding is something we should be very cautious of, according to the principles of Enlightenment. However, if our knowledge grows over time, only relying on what we know now must imply that knowledge is always partial. It is therefore irrational to claim that our enlightened knowledge is sufficient for *complete understanding* if our knowledge is always **partial**. If we accept that knowledge grows over time, we must also accept that our understanding **also** changes over time.

Our knowledge does not grow equally in relation to all types of knowledge, so the gaps in knowledge are not equally distributed across the spectrum of understanding. This may also mean that some kinds of knowledge are more accessible as **articulated evaluation** than other kinds of knowing, like feelings, intuitions and emotions. If we consider our nonverbal and relational experiences as relevant to our understanding of life, as well as our grasp of scientific knowledge, then we have to acknowledge that **articulated** 'rationality' can only apply to **some** of what there is to know. If this is accepted, it is contradictory to say that **only** knowledge which can be rationally evaluated and articulated can count towards our understanding of the world.

Nowhere is this point more starkly demonstrated than when comparing Richard Dawkins' and Dennis Alexander's views. Both are eminent scientists. However, they take very different stances when it comes to the role of chance as a determinant of life. Whereas Dawkins in *The God Delusion* talks about chance as belonging to a "deep understanding of Darwinism" [100], Alexander says that "taken as a whole, evolution is far from being a chance process".[101] One might leave the discussion there as two scientists having differing perspectives. However, we know the broader worldviews that they hold. Dawkins is an atheist, whilst Alexander is a Christian. Both attempt, as most people do, to reconcile what they know about the world with what they feel about it. Each brings together what they sense with what they know. Dawkins doesn't know that there is no God in the same way he knows about DNA: Alexander doesn't know

---

[100] *The God Delusion*, page 139
[101] *Creation or Evolution, Do We Have to Choose?* page 322

God in the same way he knows about biochemistry. They may agree on particular aspects of the science, but they have very divergent ways of interpreting the implications of what they do agree on.

Evaluating the Alternatives

> Should we use all of our experience, both scientific and relational, but at the same time remember we do not have all the answers?

We have seen that a 'rational' act such as murder may contradict a 'rational' rule, namely making murder a crime. We have also found that opposite theories, such as Dennett's view of evolution and creationist science, both have internal coherence, an essential characteristic of enkratic rationality. It is not surprising that when reading a book such as Broome's *Rationality Through Reasoning*, it is difficult to find rationality anywhere defined in a totally circumscribed way. 'Rationality' itself is a contested concept. Nevertheless, to abandon it would be to abandon an essential intellectual capability that potentially helps us to understand ourselves and the world around us. Paradoxically, we can make the best use of it once we acknowledge and accept its limitations. If our knowledge is partial, then so are the tools we have to develop it. Once we recognise this, it is easier to place the knowledge we do have into a broader context. For a believer in God, this kind of 'humility', to use a religious term, must be an essential condition if faith is not to be misused. It is contradictory to believe in God as one who knows infinitely more than we do, and at the same time believe that we know all that God is thinking. All young children think they know more than their parents, but how many of them are right? Of those who are, it is usually because the parents are in some way dysfunctional.[102]

The critical question is not how to define 'rationality', but what range of experience and knowledge we should take into account when considering such questions as to whether life is ultimately intentional or not. Secondly, the awareness that whatever we do know is partial, whether scientific, emotional, relational or spiritual, should prevent us from believing we are in possession of the truth, the whole truth and nothing but the truth. We can know part of the whole truth; this seems to apply to both human relationships and scientific enquiry. On reflection, it seems also to apply to self-knowledge.

One of the claims of evolutionists (without creation) is that the theory of natural selection has given us a model through which other forms of scientific research can be conducted. In *The God Delusion*, Richard Dawkins says that although "Darwinism may not be directly relevant to the inanimate world – cosmology, for example, it raises our consciousness in areas outside its original territory of biology".[103] This is a substantial claim and so the next chapter discusses whether the theory of evolution should be classed as a 'metatheory'.

---

[102] An unbeliever like Dawkins might say that the notion of God is dysfunctional in itself. However, for the unbeliever all this is saying is that the authors of such dysfunctional ideas are human beings.

[103] *The God Delusion*, page 139

Chapter 6
Evolution as a Metatheory – a Reassessment

The Evolutionary Gospel

Is evolution the theory which all other scientific theories should fit into? Have human beings taken over from the random forces of natural selection? If they have, is it clear where we are heading?

In 2017, Steve Jones published a short sketch of evolution for popular consumption.[104] He says this:

Evolution is the grammar of biology ... Without it, the subject would be a list of disconnected facts, as it was until 1859, when Charles Darwin published *The Origin of Species* ... His ideas led to a revolution in science and in humankind's view of itself ... it moves from the obvious to the unthinkable: from cattle breeding to the claim that 'light will be cast on man and his origins'. This statement has proved triumphantly correct.[105]

---

[104] Steve Jones was Head of the Department of Genetics, Evolution and Environment at the University College London up until 2010.
[105] *Evolution*, page 4

This is a typical modern view about evolution. Evolution has displaced many traditional ways of looking at the world and has, in fact, made belief in God redundant. More than this, evolution has, at least in the popular 'mind', become the theoretical template for science to follow. Steve Jones says this in his more academic book, *In the Blood – God, Genes and Destiny*:

> St Paul himself described the conflict between the fate of the genetic message in the body and that in the cells which transmit to the next generation ... 'For ... this mortal must put on immortality.' Biology shows how right he was: that, although the life of those who bear them is transient, the world of genes will live forever.[106]

In spite of the fact that St Paul's writings in 1 Corinthians 15 were about a lasting relationship with God beyond death and ***not*** genetics, Jones is adamant that genetics have an eternal quality. However, at the end of his explanation of millions of years of evolutionary history, Jones makes a puzzling statement about life since 1945: "Almost everyone lives long enough to have children, and most people have about the same number. As a result, ***natural selection***, which depends on differences in survival and fertility, has – at least for the time being and at least in rich countries – ***almost stopped***"(emphasis added).[107] All he says by way of explanation is that "Jumbo jets mean the days of population bottlenecks have gone".[108] This could be expanded to mean that birth control methods, affluence, intercontinental travel and immigration control are the kinds of factors which interfere

---

[106] *In the Blood – God, Genes and Destiny*, page 282
[107] *Evolution*, page 50
[108] Ibid, page 50

with natural selection. He goes on to say "language does far better than DNA and means that, uniquely, the area of human evolution has moved from body to mind … If stupidity does not destroy it, the future will see a triumph of the average as genes mix and merge. Fortunately, perhaps, none of us will be around to find out". [109]

I do not know exactly what Steve Jones means by this, but it is a startlingly confused rather than triumphant picture of history, a history which emerged from complex physical interactions to the present day where the human race could destroy itself through stupidity. There are more cogent criteria which can be employed to evaluate if evolution is worthy of the name 'metatheory', a theory within which most or all others can be accommodated. I am going to use part of a famous lecture given by Bertrand Russell at the Battersea Town Hall on Sunday March 6, 1927, where he gave his reasons for not being a Christian.[110] The arguments he put forward are sometimes used to justify the claim that the theory of evolution is all-encompassing, although Russell himself made no such claim. He was more concerned with promoting the primacy of science over religious belief; it is in that general sense that his arguments apply to this question. I will use three of the headings he used in that lecture, as they seem particularly relevant to the debate about the status of evolutionary theory.

The First Cause Argument

We always look for causes, but can that go on forever? If there was no such thing as time before the universe came about, might the question about what happened first be the wrong one?

---

[109] Ibid, page 50
[110] I will summarize his arguments. The transcript of the lecture 'Why I am not a Christian' can be found at *https://users.drew.edu/jlenz/whynot.html*

Russell came to refute the idea of there being a First Cause because it led to an infinite regress: if God made the world, then who made God? [111] He did not see the necessity to find a cause for the natural world nor to identify such a thing as a beginning; he felt that it was a lack of imagination that led to such notions as God creating the world from a standing start. There is no need to attach a cause to the natural world.

Russell's First Cause argument is often used by modern atheists to dismiss the notion of God and replace it with evolutionary theory, because the process of evolution is something we can actually track. However, the same argument applies to evolutionary theory: once the material origins of life are identified, the question arises as to what led to those elements.[112] The evolutionary case is that one thing led to another, without intent, so this would not be sufficient to give evolution a pre-eminence above other scientific explanations. Sequences do not lead back to a first cause because any first cause must have an antecedent. Evolution is necessarily confined to the calendar system of time. Consequently, Russell's argument implies that evolution was the continuation of a flow that had no original intent behind it. Evolution might be a significant marker, but it should not replace 'God' as a total explanation for life if the First Cause argument is correct.

Secondly, if Stephen Hawking's Big Bang theory is to be taken seriously, there may be a dimension where time *does not exist.* Stephen Hawking again explained this in his lecture on the Origins of the Universe in 2005. Matter and energy are themselves changeable entities from which space and time emerge: as the universe grew from

---

[111] Russell had originally come across this argument in John Stuart Mill's autobiography.

[112] Russell was writing before Stephen Hawking's Big Bang theory was published.

a point of singularity where all matter, light and energy were sucked inwards, time and space also grew outwards. However, space and time grew out from *nothing*, so it makes no sense to talk of time before the universe began. Regardless of what came *first*, **time** is no longer an overarching control factor which applies to all of nature. Time as a dimension means that there are more dimensions to follow, some of which may be currently unknown or even unknowable.[113] Russell's First Cause argument was firmly rooted to time: without time, First Cause becomes a cause which contains unknown possibilities.

The Natural Law Argument

What is really meant by a natural law? Can randomness and intent combine together and if they can, which is the stronger?

Russell explains how, in the eighteenth century, the notion of 'God' was used as if He were a puppeteer to explain natural phenomena, and scientific discoveries have now made such explanations redundant. He goes on to explain that what we often believe to be laws are in fact averages which have arisen through chance. The notion of law implies a law-giver but if they are only averages then no law-giver is required.

Russell is surely right to point out that any perception of God based on the changing face of science is bound to fail. If we think nature is simpler than it is, the attributes of God have to be readjusted when scientific knowledge expands. We change what we think God is capable of, so 'God' becomes a perceived image based on what *we*

---

[113] As already quoted on page 33 in Chapter 1, Marcus du Sautoy says, "the question of whether time had a beginning or extends infinitely into the past feels like one that will remain on the scientific books for some time yet."

know, undermining the concept of a being beyond us. It is another version of Hume's 'faces in the moon' argument. However, there is an obvious parallel that if a *particular* scientific theory is raised into a place of unassailable prominence, such elevation could also inhibit the discovery of new and vital scientific information.

There are, as Russell points out, many elements of science that *are* reliably predictable and many that are not; the latter are, as far as we can tell, random. The more random elements we find, the easier it is to think that life in the cosmos is based on chance. However, proportioning what we know into a classification of 'chance' or 'order' assumes that what we know is enough to make such a judgement. If we consider what we don't know, no such judgement is possible.

Russell talks about a confusion between human and natural laws. Evolutionists have sometimes used the same argument to say that what was thought to be intentional design is in fact the result of chemical and biological chance. However, using the theory of genetic inheritance to explain how particular relationships might develop is a similar confusion; we do not use our knowledge of interpersonal relations to explain how DNA works, so why should we use DNA to explain how relationships work?

The Argument from Design

Why is nature so chaotic if there is a designer? What are the criteria of design? When we look at the destructive aspects of human nature, should we blame God or point to the ways people misuse their freedom to exert cruelty onto their fellow humans?

Russell's chief argument against the idea of creative design resembles the evolutionary argument. We have adapted to our environment as opposed to our environment having been created for us. Russell refers to Voltaire's remark that noses were made in the shape needed for spectacles to fit over them. This is a light-hearted way of saying that we look for ways of justifying the idea of creative design in nature rather than reveal the evidence of it through scientific enquiry. A more serious criticism Russell levels against the notion of there being a God is why such an all-powerful God would produce the Ku Klux Klan or the Fascists.

The force of the argument in Chapter 3 was to raise the point that intelligent intervention by human beings in natural processes is very much a modern reality rather than a fabrication of religious imagination. So, it is possible to find intelligent designers, ourselves, and this gives rise to the question as to whether we are the only intelligent designers to have ever existed.

As far as intelligent design is concerned, the question never seems to imply anything more than the design of the natural world, although Russell is also criticising the 'design' of the human character. Designers of buildings have to decide what the purpose of their design is. Is it to house as many for as low a cost as possible? Is it to suit the individual needs of those who might live in it? Is it to provide comfort with no expense spared or is it to enhance links with the local community? For the purposes of this discussion, we have to ask what the purpose of design might be, if one is to admit any kind of logical possibility of there being a creative force behind the world. Is that purpose great art, or depth and meaning within human relationships, or the ability to farm the land and build shelter? Is it the establishment of mutually supportive communities or, to put a very modern criteria into the mix, individual freedom? Without establishing the criteria of design, the question of why the world is designed the way it is, is too general a question to analyse.

It is also important to remember that if scientific knowledge is partial, any assessment of whether something is a product of a mind or not has to be provisional. Domasio, an atheist, when discussing the origins of life in *The Strange Order of Things*, puts the issue like this: "Well-groomed metabolism – that is, metabolism guided by homeostasis – would define the beginnings of life and its movement forward would be the driving force of evolution. Natural selection ... did the rest, which included centralised metabolic regulation and replication." [114]

The argument is that the forces of natural selection needed a stable, self-regulating platform from which to launch themselves. Immediately there is a tension in biological terms between self-regulation and the blind struggle for survival, both of which are needed for life to begin. Judgements about the 'design' element of creation will significantly reduce if only the latter is considered.

However, when it comes to Fascism and racial terror, it is, of course, fair enough to ask why a God would allow such things to occur. Any answer can seem trite; the question is too profound for a formulaic answer. For Russell, however, the question of why the scientific community has not found a solution to such ills must also reflect on the limitations of science itself. The in-principle question implied by the 'Why did God create the Ku Klux Klan and Fascists?' is not unlike asking why parents who have almost complete power over their new-born babies are unable to raise them into perfect children. The answer is obviously complex, but one essential element of child rearing is to encourage independence at an appropriate age. As independence is gained, the power of the parent in controlling the offspring's behaviour is diminished. Relationships, if they are to be genuine, have to include elements of freedom and choice.

A summary of the three arguments

---

[114] *The Strange Order of Things*, page 41

Russell's first two arguments can be applied to evolution in the same way Russell applied them to belief in God. The First Cause argument can be used against any theory that has a beginning, whether intended or accidental: whatever the start, there is always an antecedent.

Secondly, evolution is not lawlike because there is an uneven and sometimes changing balance between regulation and randomness within chemical and biological processes. More significantly, the power of artificial selection is now a critical factor which counteracts natural selection. If I decide to cross-breed flowers, design chemical weapons, clear large areas of rain forest or develop stem cell research, what law am I keeping?

The Argument from Design Russell uses is one often employed by evolutionists (without creation). Design theories are flawed by the uncovering of processes that contain random elements and so the replacement theory is seen as pre-eminent. This argument is mistaken because even if there is no God, discovering the mechanism of evolution does not in itself make it a pre-eminent theory. Evolution is *only* one of at least three major archetypes, quantum theory, the general theory of relativity and natural selection. If I am a very clever detective and can solve a particularly difficult crime, this does not mean that I will be able to solve all crimes.

The Implications

> Where will human beings take the theory of evolution? What does it mean for artificial selection to take over from natural selection?

If artificial selection becomes the key variable in assessing the risk of our species surviving in the next millennia and beyond, human intent will overtake natural selection as the dominant force in question. The history of evolution will change from the power of natural forces into the power of human decision making. The question of whether there is a creative power behind our life will mean more than trying to equate it with the knowledge we have about the origins of life and species development. It will be more about whether we have anyone, apart from ourselves, to seek advice from as to how to manage our own survival.

The universe grew from a highly dense mass of neurons and protons, initially forming hydrogen and helium and then expanding into stars which formed other heavier elements through the means of a cooling process. The origins of the universe are also the origins of space and time. Eventually on earth the conditions came about where inorganic elements reacted with each other to form the simplest forms of organic life. From there on, natural selection led to the eventual arrival of human beings. Those human beings are developing the capacity to manipulate the natural world around them, including their own genetic makeup. Now that power of manipulation has a wider implication for the human species, how should we use it to achieve what Russell describes as a good world?

If God has not produced the Ku Klux Klan or the Fascists, then we have. Russell says we need knowledge, kindliness and courage. Can the theory of evolution inspire us to use our increasing knowledge in a kinder and more courageous way? Can we derive a sense of spirituality from our understanding of natural selection? The next chapter looks at this issue from an analytical rather than an experiential perspective and the following chapter includes a discussion of whether the removal of religion might be sufficient to set the human race on a more positive course.

Chapter 7
Immanence and Evolution – are they compatible?

Can the theory of evolution help us decipher the meaning of life?

Modern approaches to seeking meaning and purpose in life often incorporate evolution as the springboard for working out those aspirations.[115] I am going to consider three different ways of justifying the theory of evolution through the application of immanence. Immanence in this chapter does not refer to the meaning of an inherent characteristic, or an event about to happen (imminence), but to the claim that the study of being and any theory of knowledge should properly be confined to anything directly accessible within the human mind and spirit. It specifically **excludes** any belief in a transcendent God. The shift towards immanence, away from traditional transcendent perspectives which infer the existence of a God outside of space and time, is generally considered to be derived from the insights Darwin's theory of evolution brought forward. As Verhoef says, "In the religion science discourse religion is understood as the product of normal evolutionary processes".[116] To put it another

---

[115] Sometimes the word 'spirituality' is used to convey 'purpose'. It is important to note that those who reject the notion of a transcendent God still positively seek a meaningful sense of spirituality for themselves.

[116] *Acta Academia,* Vol. 45, No. 4, page 177

way, as our knowledge of the natural world changes, so does our understanding of religion.

Evolution is a theory primarily about how species development is caused by the interaction of biological changes with changes in geological, environmental and climatic conditions.[117] It is the most widely held explanation in Western democratic society of how the human species has arrived at its present point. It has provided the impetus for the contemporary preference for immanence as a theory of understanding the human condition, basing itself on the way scientific advances, particularly Darwin's theory of natural selection, have replaced the need for a belief in an external transcendent force. Once the magician's technique is laid bare, the magic is no more, and so there is also no magician.

Immanence stems from empirical discoveries in both the natural and human sciences. It is a set of theories of understanding or non-understanding (i.e. establishing the limits and status of thought and other inner experiences) which range from an emphasis on reason, to a focus on aesthetics and ethical issues, to the dismantling of meaning in language on which identity and intention is based. Immanence, in this sense, can include both scientific theories as well as the existential study of being, provided no assumption resting on any revelation from a transcendent divine Godhead or other metaphysical entity is made.

I will examine how three particular modes of immanence apply to the theory of evolution and explore whether they are compatible with each other. Even though the theory of evolution gave rise

---

[117] It is important to recognise that evolutionists do not claim that random genetic mutations apply to all such interactions between living entities and the external environment through successive generations; for example, animals and plants have different mechanisms to bacteria for exchanging DNA. (See page 328 in *The Greatest Show on Earth, The Evidence for Evolution*)

to the modern preference for immanence in the study of being, paradoxically, immanence itself, in any one or combination of the three forms I will explore, is not fully suited to explaining evolution itself. In other words, it is perfectly possible to work out a 'spiritual' meaning using the theory of evolution, but those meanings do not, on their own, lead us back to evolution itself. I am using the word 'spirituality' here in the sense of something everyone explores whether through organised religious activity or elsewhere: it is the search for our own vital essence.

Kant and Reason

> Immanuel Kant, who died four years before Darwin was born, distinguished between two kinds of knowledge: mathematical knowledge and the knowledge we gain from observation. Had Kant known about the theory of evolution, which of these would he have considered to be the best fit with the theory?

I will start by exploring a Kantian perspective on immanence, a perspective which examines the scope and limits of reason. Levi Bryant summarises Kant's view of the way our minds work in saying that "objects conform to the mind rather than the mind to objects".[118] Kant felt that Hume's radical dismantling of the scientific method, where the notion of causality was called into doubt, required reassessment. He, therefore, devised a limiting case for the use of reason in interpreting our experience of life and the natural world around us. The limit he placed on the use of reason was that it should only be used to interpret information directly accessible to us rather

---

[118] *Difference and Givenness; Deleuze's Transcendental Empiricism and the Ontology of Immanence*, page 2

than to speculate about metaphysical possibilities beyond the reach of our comprehension. This is the principle which evolutionists (without creation) adopt in exploring all aspects of life.

Kant was at pains to demonstrate that reason explains how *we experience* the world, rather than describing what the world *is actually like*. Fundamentally, there is a ready-made framework in our minds which our sensory experiences fit into. Kant called a pivotal element of this framework "a priori synthetic" judgements.[119] Geometry in particular was the archetypal subject which Kant used to explain what "a priori synthetic" judgements are. So, for example, an astronomer can observe how planets move in relation to the sun and then record and comment on what has been observed. Underpinning our understanding of these planetary movements are mathematical and geometric formulae; for Kant, those formulae exist independently of any observations of planetary movement,[120] and that is what makes them "a priori", logical connections which combine to provide a framework into which empirical, or "a posteriori" information as

---

[119] These "a priori synthetic" statements remain true in all possible worlds, and therefore cannot be contradicted by empirical evidence. That is why they are called "a priori". A simple example he used was $5+7=12$. In Kant's view, this was a statement which no amount of evidence could overturn. The term synthetic refers to a combination of two distinct entities (5 and 7), which result in an entity which is different from either of the first two (12). Although Jean Piaget's theory of concept development could be said to be akin to Kant's view of the mind in terms of our inbuilt potential for cognitive functioning, Piaget would not agree that synthetic "a priori" judgements are mental constructs independent of our sensory experience. He would argue that numbers are learnt through concrete experience.

[120] The contradiction in Kant's position was that there could be "a priori" judgements independent of our experience, but simultaneously those judgements form a crucial part of how our minds interpret the world. This was the basis for Willard Quine's attack on the existence of an autonomous rationality, one which claims to be somehow separate but also part of the human mind.

Kant called it, could be placed.[121] Empirical science is a legitimate subject of study, but, for Kant, subject areas which **primarily** rely on empirical observations do not provide the same security as those *also* based on "a priori" synthetic judgements. So, in exploring what he might have thought about evolution, it is important to identify which aspects of the theory might apply in all possible worlds and which are based on empirical discoveries.[122]

Kant believed that our minds have an internal framework in relation to space and time, into which all *experiences* fit. Time and space belong to the "a priori" category. Robert Wicks, in his book, *Kant, A Complete Introduction,* says:

Empty space and empty time are conceivable, and moreover, are such that we must conceive of them *as the very conditions* under which we can have any experience at all. With such reflections, Kant maintains that space and time are within us[123] before we experience any objects.[124] (emphasis original)

I want to suggest that Kant's view of the theory of evolution would have been based on "a priori" judgements about space and time, and "a posteriori" or empirical information about the tree of cousinship,[125]

---

[121] The Latin for 'a priori' means 'from before' whilst 'a posteriori' means 'from the latter': it is the difference between theoretical deduction and forming ideas from observations.

[122] *Kant , A complete introduction*, pages 57-59. The original sources of this argument can be found in the second edition(1787) of Kant's '*Critique of Pure Reason*' on pages 16 and 41.

[123] Carlo Rovelli points out in *The Order of Time* that Kant distinguishes between space and time, space being "shaped by our *external* sense" and time "by our way of ordering internal states *within* ourselves", page 159, emphasis original.

[124] *Kant , A complete introduction*, page 56

[125] This refers to the resemblances between species which can be traced back to common ancestors.

the tracking of neutral mutations,[126] and fossil evidence. Time is an integral part of evolution itself, as random mutations which are best suited to cope with external changes in a plant or animal's environment are selected through ***successive generations.*** Time, in Kantian terms, is the immovable framework in which random mutations can flourish.

Kant's view of the empirical evidence was also clear. As the commentator on Kant, Norman Kemp-Smith says, "Even so called dead matter is not merely inert. By its inherent powers of gravity and chemical attraction it spontaneously gives rise to the most wonderful forms".[127] Kant distinguished between the "blindly working laws" which both maintain and account for the origin of the planetary system, and the "internal self-developing power" of living forms of life.[128]

Kant's position is in sympathy with the theory of evolution, from an empirical or "a posteriori" perspective. However, "a priori" synthetic judgements which are mirrored by mathematical laws are not fully compatible with the retrospective methods through which the theory of evolution has been deduced. Dawkins, in *The Greatest Show on Earth*, says, "Evolutionary scientists are in the position

---

[126] These are changes in genetic structure which are "undetectable by natural selection, but detectable by molecular geneticists; and that is an ideal combination for an evolutionary clock." Taken from *The Greatest Show on Earth, The Evidence for Evolution*, page 334

[127] *A Commentary to Kant's 'Critique of Pure Reason'*, page 539

[128] Ibid, page 539. It is worth pointing out that evolutionists do not seek to present the theory of evolution as able to evidence the origin of life. Richard Dawkins says, in *The Greatest Show on Earth*, "We have no evidence about what the first step in making life was, but we do know the kind of step it must have been. It must have been whatever it took to get natural selection started … And that means the key step was the arising, by some process yet unknown, of a self-replicating entity", page 419.

of detectives who come late to the scene of the crime".[129] Species development is traced by looking back at both random genetic mutation and adaptation to changing environments and therefore it is not possible to predict its future course. It is the **random element** of genetic mutation which prohibits the precise **predictive quality** which, in Kant's view, mathematical laws possess. He thought that mathematical "a priori" calculations were the highest form of knowledge as they, in his view, work in any context.

Kant and Materialism

> Would Kant have changed his mind about 'time' in the light of quantum theory? How would this have affected his view of evolution as a basis for inspiration?

Had he lived today, Kant would have no doubt deliberated on modern ways of changing biological and environmental conditions. IVF treatment for infertility, gender reassignment surgery and the knowledge of how human activity can affect climate change were not contemporary concerns when Kant was writing in the 1800s. They are, however, clear examples of how the human 'mind' can be used in the manipulation of physical processes, or as Dawkins might classify it, "artificial selection".[130] So, if Kant were asked which is the dominant force, human intention or biological processes, what might he say? I propose that he'd say human cognition is **only** more likely to be dominated by biological processes in the context of evolutionary theory **if** time can be shown to be an absolutely fixed constant, an "a priori" truth. This is because unpredictable changes happen within a

---

[129] *The Greatest Show on Earth, The Evidence for Evolution*, page 85
[130] *The Greatest Show on Earth, The Evidence for Evolution*, page 39

fixed "a priori" backdrop: the unpredictability of biological random mutations leading to the emergence of cognition is circumscribed by the fixed law of time.

Should Kant have been able to fast forward to the present day, he would also have taken into account research findings into particle movement and gravitational forces. Carlo Rovelli summarises where research has currently arrived at in his recent book, *Seven Brief Lessons in Physics*.

The heat of black holes is like the Rosetta Stone of physics, written in a combination of three languages – Quantum, Gravitational and thermodynamic – still awaiting decipherment in order to reveal the true nature of time.[131]

Despite the outstanding unknowns[132], we are much more certain now that time is held **within** the universe and not **outside** it, as Kant imagined it to be. If time is a relative dimension, then, by implication, evolution has to follow. Kant's view of time, in today's world, would have been forced to shift from the fixed "a priori" model towards the empirically based "a posteriori" model, in the light of its changeable nature through variations in gravitational forces. The theory of evolution would, therefore, be more likely to be described by Kant as "a posteriori" knowledge whilst the mathematical calculations of quantum theory would be classed as "a priori". If this were the case, Kant would have been unlikely to use the theory of evolution as a

---

[131] *Seven Brief Lessons in Physics*, page 62
[132] These unknowns appear to be growing rather than reducing: the debate over the rate of expansion of the universe is an example. Dark energy and dark matter discussions carry a health warning as to how much is unknown. The website https://science.nasa.gov/astrophysics/focus-areas/what-is-dark-energy says of Dark Energy that "More is unknown than is known".

spiritual springboard. If he were to seek inspiration from science, he would veer towards theories which were mathematically based and confirmed through observation: quantum theories would figure high on the list.

Kant, however, was not a simple materialist, and did recognise the difference between human intent and organic processes. He was equally concerned with aesthetics and ethics as with the theory of knowledge and did not assume that all human cognitive behaviour is the product of some kind of deterministic process. It is not clear whether Kant's writings in total provide a formulation as to how organic processes and human intentionality can merge into one resolution, but his principle of how the mind organises itself creates a solution.

In Kant's view, the apparent incompatibility between mechanism and teleology is not situated objectively in nature itself, as if the world were absurd. The conflict is internal to us, and it concerns how our mind projects two opposing ways to comprehend nature as a system.[133]

Kant wrote a great deal about human intent: his view of morality, as Wicks says, is driven by "respect for ourselves as rational, and hence as law-formulating, legislating beings".[134] Kant believed, even though it was impossible to find a proof for the existence of God, that we should "examine the world around us *as if* it were the product of a supreme intelligence".[135] This would be sufficient motivation for us to be openminded and expand our knowledge of the world.

---

[133] *A Commentary to Kant's 'Critique of Pure Reason'*, page 209 (Kemp-Smith)
[134] *Kant , A complete introduction*, page 151
[135] Ibid, page 132

In the end, we should "act independently of sensuous interests and personal inclinations, for these have nothing to do with, and are indeed subject to, what we timelessly are as law-giving beings".[136] It can be seen that to derive a spirituality from an evolutionary theory that is intimately tied up with earthy, chaotic and sometimes brutal interactions is something far removed from Kant's rarefied vision of human fulfilment through pure reason.[137]

The Embodiment of Religion in Humankind – Verhoef

> If evolution has fashioned the human species from the simplest forms of life, then our spiritual awareness should also have developed and matured – is it possible to trace the DNA of meaning and spirituality?

A different form of immanence is the perspective taken by Verhoef, who claims there is a self- evident need for human beings to live in aesthetic and moral ways. How does Verhoef fit this narrative into the evolutionary perspective? Verhoef says:

> One way is to rethink the entire concept of religion itself and to move away from an ontological transcendence to the immanence of the human body. God is then not outside or above human beings or this world but reduced to certain experiences within the human body emotionally and rationally.[138]

---

[136] Ibid, page 154
[137] Kant's view of the role of reason has similarities with Stephen Pinker's New Enlightenment Project which will be discussed in Chapter 9.
[138] *Acta Academia,* Vol. 45, No. 4, page 175

This view of immanence does not discard the experience of religious and spiritual insight but transfers belief in an external God into the mysterious depths of our psyche, into the light, shade and darkness of our own inner lives. For Verhoef, "self-transcendence ... locates itself in the immanent".[139]

I want to apply evolutionary theory to those faculties which underpin conscious religious, aesthetic and moral experience. To address this, a starting point might be through exploring the notion of reciprocity in non-human species. The idea is that reciprocity is a necessary condition for the application of moral judgements in human society even though co-operative behaviour in itself does not imply moral activity. If mutually beneficial activity can be identified within and between non-human species, one could look for an evolutionary thread leading to the eventual flourishing of human immanent reflection.

Tim Clutton-Brock summarises research findings in the following way:

> Explanations of cooperation between non-kin in animal societies often suggest that individuals exchange resources or services and that cooperation is maintained by reciprocity. But do cooperative interactions between unrelated individuals in non-human animals really resemble exchanges or are they a consequence of simpler mechanisms? Firm evidence of reciprocity in animal societies is rare and many examples of cooperation between non-kin probably represent cases of intra-specific mutualism or manipulation.[140]

---

[139] Ibid, page 178
[140] *Nature*, Vol 462, November 2009, page 51

It seems mistaken to assume that non-human animals are any more manipulative than humans, while the variety of species where elements of mutualism, manipulation or cooperation have been identified is much wider than commonly understood and not at all confined to primates. This supports the notion that the roots of conscious, reflective and socially interactive behaviour in humans could be traced much further back than the relatively recent beginnings of human civilisation. There are, nevertheless, critical differences between the findings from animal studies and the nature of human society. Clutton-Brock says the key difference between humans and other animals is the ability to plan for future co-operative actions: "lacking the ability to make specific arrangements about future events, other animals may commonly be restricted to cooperative strategies that generate immediate benefits to their inclusive fitness".[141]

It is clear that the emergence of consciousness, social interaction and human investigative intelligence have combined to make the human species into a dominant force amongst other species and with it an ability to mould the environment rather than be moulded by it. Neuro-philosopher Professor Patricia Churchland, writing in the New Scientist, says "if you want to be a big learner, you need to be a social creature – and that brings you to the doorstep of morality".[142] With these capabilities, it is not surprising that a quest for meaning and significance has also arisen. The difficulty lies in establishing a credible evolutionary *thread* which can be traced in terms of *social interaction and reciprocity* rather than adaptation to

---

[141] Ibid, pages 55-56
[142] *New Scientist, Vol. 243, No,3249, September 2019*, page 46

environmental changes based on fossil evidence.[143] Domasio makes it clear in 'The Strange Order of Things' that "we do not descend directly from bacteria or social insects" [144], but he does say this: "our current lives and their cultural objects and practices can be linked, albeit not easily, to the lives of yore, before there were feelings and subjectivity, before there were words and decisions. Here and there one can find a guiding thread ... The task of biology, psychology and philosophy is to make the thread continuous".[145] Professor Churchland points to an evolutionary chain of mammalian warm bloodedness which improved energy storage and the capacity to be more flexible in managing environments. The "genetic trick" [146] of oxytocin moving from the body to the brain is, she says, what led to mammals and birds becoming maternally protective. This interaction then broadened out into a wider moral compass, firstly into small primitive communities and later into the more explicit moral debate in contemporary society.

From an evolutionary perspective, it is worth asking the rhetorical question as to why the human species is the only species to have taken such a **significant advantage** of "language (and associated psychological capacities)", given the power those capacities give us over other dominant species.[147] This is particularly the case given Domasio's

---

[143] See Table 1 on page 54 of Tim Clutton-Brock's article. The table includes fish, birds, ungulates, deer, carnivores, bats and primates. Dawkins' chapter on the "Tree of Cousinship" in The Greatest Show on Earth demonstrates that the variety of species involved does not preclude the possibility of finding a traceable lineage; however, it is much more problematic to trace the heritage of moral interaction because, as Dawkins says, "hair and language don't fossilize well" page 187.

[144] The Strange Order of Things, page 24

[145] Ibid, page 243

[146] New Scientist, Vol. 243, No,3249, September 2019, page 46

[147] Nature, Vol 462,November 2009, page 55 (Clutton-Brock). I have no view but think it is a valid question in the context of natural selection.

account of ants and bees, 100 million years ago, being able to "divide labor intelligently within the group to deal with the problems of finding energy resources, transform them into products useful for their lives, and manage the flow of those products".[148] It is relevant to ask: why have these capacities not been built on in the way Churchland describes through natural selection in the many intervening generations? The emergence of more than one species capable of abstract thought would have made for a very different world.

Beyond Being – Deleuze

For some modern thinkers like Gilles Deleuze, the ways we understand the world never reveal the true picture which lies behind our words. That world is ever changing, impersonal and chaotic. Is it beyond our grasp?

Whereas Kant's and Verhoef's approaches to immanence rely on an underpinning rationalism, Deleuze and his predecessor, Henri Bergson, seek to overturn this assumption as the basis for a theory of knowledge, replacing it with a view of reality that centres on a lack of order, purpose or finality. This does not mean that scientific laws are fabrications, but it does, for them, imply that science and its reliance on repetition, regularity and prediction, is an intermediary or pragmatic tool rather than a complete explanation of reality. Marc Rölli explains how Deleuze would have spoken about immanence.

Ultimately for Deleuze, the apparently opaque concept of being dissolves into a multitude of differential processes, singularities

---

[148] *The Strange Order of Things*, page 23

and events. The concept of being that suggests stability, unity, grounding and order evaporates *as difference* into the plurality of becoming. This becoming that occurs immanently – in other words, that structures itself – is for Deleuze nothing else than time. Thus the realm of microphysics and floating quanta cannot be separated from the immanent environment; it is not located somewhere beyond the subject but on "this side of consciousness" (as Hegel would say), as a process which is differential as much as genetic, and which constitutes experience.[149](emphasis original)

If our discoveries of the disordered and impenetrable layers of the physical world are correct, then we ourselves are ultimately the same. What we should do is be honest and let the 'chaos' enter into our own self-awareness of being; science should suspend the priority it gives to order because it is not on course to discover some kind of master process (the master *plan* of transcendence has already been abandoned as transcendence has been superseded by immanence). The implication is that the theory of evolution should be held as **one** kind of differential process, not the **determining** process of all others.[150] There is no **order** of intelligible knowledge, just a mix of events, processes and theories which we find ourselves in the middle of; the quest for a permanent sense of identity in this context is mistaken. Our acceptance of this chaos is curiously the place where we might find security. This entry from the *Stanford Encyclopaedia of Philosophy* illustrates the point.

---

[149] *Bulletin de la Societé Américaine de Philosophie de Langue Français*, Vol. 14, No. 2, Fall 2004, page 67

[150] When evolution is used as a determining process, it has a symmetry with the modern atheistic view of traditional transcendence. The idea of a supernatural God was discarded in favour of the substituted theory of evolution, but all this amounts to is a transfer of the characteristics of God into the forces of nature.

Deleuze and Guattari ... extend the notion of self-organizing material systems – those with no need of transcendent organizing agents such as gods, leaders, capital, or subjects – to the social, linguistic, political-economic, and psychological realms. [151]

The emergence of the theory of evolution implied science was the new 'deity', and this led to immanence as a means of understanding reality as opposed to reliance on an external Godhead. Philosophers who espouse Deleuze's approach consider that *symbolic representation* of the inner self is something deeper than scientific knowledge, even though science is sufficient reason to preclude a belief in a transcendent God. Verhoef says:

With his notion of pure immanence, he (Deleuze) wishes to move beyond the dualism of form-matter that brings with it a transcendent judgement of mind over matter ... For Deleuze this immanent life is impersonal. [152]

Verhoef points out that Deleuze could be accused of creating an orthodoxy of 'chaos', where judgements are made as to whether someone is holding onto a value when they should let go of it. It would be like an anarchist's one commandment, 'The minute you believe in anything with certainty, discard it.' A defence of Deleuze's 'plane of immanence', as it is referred to, might be that the process of distinguishing between the 'superiority' of language against the primacy of the physical universe of which human thought is only a small part, necessarily requires a

---

[151] Go to https://plato.stanford.edu/entries/deleuze/ which takes you to 'Gilles Deleuze', then to Section 4, 'Collaboration with Guattari' and then to 4.2 'A Thousand Plateaus'
[152] *Acta Academia*, Vol. 45, No. 4, pages 184-5

critical approach. A more telling criticism of Deleuze could be that his dismantling of the supremacy of human concept making is carried out by using language itself, an archetype of concept making.

This form of immanence here allows or even "calls one to be creatively ethical".[153] This notion of being set free from previous shackles has an echo in Jung's "teleology of the unconscious becoming progressively conscious as the core meaning of personal and collective history".[154] As each society realized that the purpose of its religion was to create an antidote for its own ills, an emerging realisation of how the unconscious symbolism of religion had served as a signpost towards a more progressive and harmonious collective would take place. This is not what Deleuze was aiming for: there is no destination as a whole. Immanence is purely a continual release from ways of thinking and acting that are embedded into our minds by repetition. It is an infinite regress where there are, in theory, no fixed points of reference.

Concluding Remarks

For Deleuze and thinkers like him, there is no final point we will reach in our understanding. Would Verhoef's argument be stronger if the equivalent to a 'fossil record' could be found for meaning and spirituality? Is the problem that the two languages (science and immanence) are different and translation from one to the other is opaque?

---

153 Ibid, page 185
154 *Difference and Givenness; Deleuze's Transcendental Empiricism and the Ontology of Immanence*, page 76

One of my aims throughout the book has been to explore the issues which arise once belief in a transcendent God is abandoned: the ontological alternatives are not straightforward to assess, at least dispassionately, and do not naturally flow back towards evolution.

I began this chapter by referring to how the theory of evolution has triggered the modern preference for immanence in the study of being and theory of knowledge. In summary, evolution, for Kant, is an intermediate theory that is not fully lawlike or mathematical; for Verhoef, it is the explanation of species development which allows for the 'evolution' of belief from transcendence to immanence; and finally, for Deleuze, it is a time-bound theory which helps to focus on the material nature of life but creates a superficial pattern and expectation of material order. It is at once clear that these three approaches to immanence are very different one from another. The Kantian approach asserts how the mind makes sense of reality but also contains a hierarchy of certainty in the ways the mind works. For Verhoef, immanence circumscribes the anthropological limits of our exploration into aesthetics and morality. Deleuzian immanence involves the absorption of materialism into consciousness without order or teleology. For Verhoef and Kant, Deleuze's position is too far removed from the full spectrum of human experience to warrant acceptance. But for Deleuze, Verhoef and Kant are subject to a misapprehension that they are dealing with reality.

Immanence is a contestable concept and the theory of evolution has not opened the door unequivocally to explain our own experience of consciousness. One possible reason for this is because the theory of evolution is **not** about the study of being, it is a theory of species development. The notion of consciousness and the accompanying heights of human achievement in art, music, science and other fields can be explained, in evolutionary terms, as a natural consequence of us being higher social animals. Alternatively, for Deleuze, there is no need to explain being, as our consciousness and conceptual explanations are the surface of a volcano of chaotic materialistic activity. Our attempts to explain anything are essentially attempts to make sense out of chaos. The ability to articulate such reflective curiosity appears to be contradictory with this conclusion but critical analysis itself is an intermediate device in this deconstructionist approach.

Either being a higher social animal or explaining consciousness as a consequence of making sense out of disorder may be arguable in the context of explaining how immanence has been derived from evolution. However, to be rigorous, it is clear the core elements of evolutionary theory are **not** capable of forming an immovable mathematical formula which states that immanence is the only option in the pursuit of the study of being.[155] So, what has led to the theory of evolution being the benchmark from which the modern preference for immanence has arisen? One possibility may be that the *symbolic* nature of the theory of evolution has enabled philosophers to depart from traditional transcendent approaches to Being, rather than the scientific content of the theory itself.[156]

The book started with an exploration as to what could count as knowledge. The mind as a physically based decision making entity was basis of a discussion about creativity, both divine and human. In examining the scope and limits of rationality, it became clear that 'rationality' is a very useful tool but not one that can give a single

---

[155] This is irrespective of the difficulty in forming an agreed definition as to what 'immanence' is.

[156] I am using 'symbolic' here to suggest that evolution has been seen by some thinkers as justification to dismiss the need for a transcendent God. However, a closer examination of immanence, as defined in this paper, and evolution shows the former does not derive its significance from the latter in any scientific sense.

view of life. Evolution as a contender for that 'single view' was not strong enough – deriving a sense of meaning and purpose from it is not straightforward. This is where the discussion has reached so far.

In the next chapter, the sceptical view of faith is explored in greater depth. For many, belief in a transcendent divine intelligence is still perceived as being self-comforting, mythically satisfying and culturally reinforcing. It is followed by a discussion about Stephen Pinker's claim that reason is the best hope for humankind. The book concludes with two chapters on where spaces for faith in a transcendent God can be found.

Chapter 8
Faith – a Catalyst for Oppression?

Historical Accuracy

> Was Christ a real person? How does research into ancient documents and archaeology help us?

As already noted in Chapter 1, articulating emotions is altogether problematic when it comes to re-experiencing a specific moment or uniquely sharing that experience with others. What kind of knowledge is belief in a personal God? It relates to our feelings, emotions and intuitions but can also be debated and contested in terms of fact or fable. Bertrand Russell, in his lecture "Why I am not a Christian", included reference to the historical facts. He cast doubt on whether Christ ever existed at all and claimed that even if he did we know nothing about him.[157] This claim is a statement of articulated belief, so it is perfectly possible to evaluate it and examine its validity. Here it is only possible to give a very brief snapshot of the kind of evaluation which can be carried out. Russell Blackford and Udo Schuklenk say this in their book, *50 Great Myths about Atheism*: "The fact is that we have almost no nonbiblical sources dating from the first century CE that even mention Jesus, let alone describe his miracles and the resurrection. There are two

---

[157] For the full text go to *https://users.drew.edu/jlenz/whynot.html*

passages in the work of the Jewish historian Flavius Josephus…and one is generally believed by scholars to have been significantly redacted at a later date to suit Christian theological interests." [158]

Blackford and Schuklenk do not refer to William Whiston's translation of and Paul Maier's commentary on Josephus (37 AD – circa 100 AD), published fourteen years prior to their own commentary. Whiston and Maier point out that there is general scholarly agreement that one of Josephus' entries regarding Jesus *was* interpolated, that is, embellished at a later date. [159] The reason, however, why scholars believe this is because of "the newly discovered Agapian text which shows no sign of interpolation … which accords well with his (i.e. Josephus') grammar and vocabulary elsewhere." [160] Whiston and Maier quote the Agapian text in full, as follows.

About this time lived Jesus, a wise man, if indeed one ought to call him a man. For he was an achiever of extraordinary deeds and was a teacher of those who accept the truth gladly. He won over many Jews and many of the Greeks. He was the Messiah. When he was indicted by the principal men among us and Pilate condemned him to be crucified, those who had come to love him originally did not cease to do so; for he appeared to them on the third day restored to life, as the prophets of the Deity had foretold these and countless other marvellous things about him. And the tribe of Christians, so named after him, has not disappeared to this day. [161]

---

[158] *50 Great Myths about Atheism*, page 172
[159] Book 18 Chapter 3.
[160] *The Revised and Expanded Edition of the New Complete Works of Josephus*, pages 662-3
[161] Ibid, page 662

The issue of interpolation is redundant in the light of the Agapian text. Maier's commentary summarises the position, "The weight of evidence, then, strongly suggests that Josephus mentioned Jesus in both passages.[162] He did so in a manner totally congruent with the New Testament portrait of Jesus, and his description, from the vantage point of a non-Christian, seems remarkably fair, particularly in view of his known proclivity for roasting false messiahs as the sorts who misled the people and brought on the Romans." [163]

Frederick Fyvie Bruce was a Professor of Biblical Criticism and Exegesis at Manchester University from 1959 to 1978. He was an avowed evangelical Christian but also someone who recognised that historical accuracy, as far as it can be established, is an integral part of faith in Christ. He comments on the reason why first century classical literature references to Christianity are weak.[164]

---

[162] Book 20, Chapter 9. The death of Jesus' brother, James.

[163] *The Revised and Expanded Edition of the New Complete Works of Josephus*, page 663 Richard Dawkins, in his recent book *Outgrowing God*, quotes this same passage from Josephus, claiming that most scholars believe it to be a later "Christian forgery" because someone like Josephus, a devout Jew, would have made "a big song and dance" about it if he had really believed that Jesus was the Messiah (pages 19-20). Dawkins' account is, at least, superficial because Josephus led anything but a settled life. After failing to overcome the Roman army in AD 66, he escaped to a cave with forty others. Being one of two remaining survivors, he managed to win the favour, the Roman commander. He moved to Rome taking on the family name of the Emperor and became known as Flavius Josephus. Writing in Rome it is unlikely that he would have made "a big song and dance" about it. Dawkins also makes no reference to the Agapian text.

[164] Josephus was a Jewish historian whom Bruce differentiates from the classical sources, by which he means non-Jewish documentation. Together with the Mishnah (Jewish jurisprudence assembled in the second century after the fall of Jerusalem in AD 70), the writings of Josephus certainly do provide external references confirming the existence of early Christianity. FF Bruce's analysis presents a much more complicated picture than Blackford and Shuklenk suggest.

From the standpoint of imperial Rome, Christianity in the first hundred years of its existence was an obscure, disreputable, vulgar oriental superstition, and if it found its way into official records at all these would have been police records, which (in common with many other first century documents that we should like to see) have disappeared.[165]

Whether Russell would have been convinced by Bruce's detailed research is a matter for conjecture, but clearly there is a very detailed and robust case to answer.[166] Research into the historicity of Jesus is not just confined to investigating ancient documents. Kristen Romey, writing in *National Geographic* in December 2017, posed Russell's question again.

Might it be possible that Jesus Christ never existed, that the whole stained glass story is pure invention? It's an assertion that's championed by some outspoken skeptics – but not, I discovered, by scholars, particularly archaeologists, whose work tends to bring flights of fancy down to literal earth.[167]

How can archaeology help? Romey cites the example of an argument that has been put forward by sceptics that there were no synagogues in Galilee until decades after Jesus' death. As construction on a retreat for pilgrims was about to begin in 2009, "archaeologists from the Israel Antiquities Authority showed up to survey the site, as required by law. After a few weeks of probing the rocky soil, they were startled to discover the buried ruins of a synagogue from the time of Jesus – the first such

---

[165] *The New Testament Documents, Are They Reliable?* Page 92
[166] A scholarly refutation of FF Bruce's *New Testament Documents: Are They Reliable?* would benefit anyone wishing to support an atheist perspective. I have not been able to find one.
[167] *National Geographic*, Vol 232,No.6, 2017, page 42

structure unearthed in Galilee. If those skeptics were right, their claim would shred the Gospel's portrait of Jesus as a faithful synagogue goer." [168] Romey concludes by saying that "to sincere believers, the scholars' quest for the historical, non-supernatural Jesus is of little consequence. That quest will be endless, full of shifting theories, unanswerable questions, irreconcilable facts. But for true believers, their faith in the life, death and Resurrection of the Son of God will be evidence enough." [169] Whereas facts are tested evidentially, faith is tested in an experiential and relational context. For those who exercise faith, it is their emotional and spiritual antennae which are essential in a world where they trust God is watching over them but cannot predict what will happen next in their lives. There are some parallels between this exercise of faith and the way a small child perceives a parent who has died early. Ultimately, that relationship experience does also depend for the believer on God's actual existence being true.

Religious Abuse

> Is religion the core problem when it comes to looking at the abuse perpetrated in the darker periods of history? Or is there a vulnerability in most of us which can be exploited by the unscrupulous?

This private exercise of faith seems a long way from the catalogue of abuse carried out in the name of religion cited by Dawkins in *The God Delusion* and Christopher Hitchens in 'god is not Great'.[170] The

---

[168] Ibid, page 64
[169] Ibid, page 68
[170] This is derived from a statement inscribed by Saddam Hussein on the Iraqi flag. Hitchens has changed the capital 'G' to a lower case 'g'.

accusation is that religious beliefs are means to brainwash people and even abuse them. There is no question that deeply abusive practices have been carried out in the name of religion throughout the ages. However, the argument is taken yet further: it is suggested that atheists like Joseph Stalin were copying the brutality of previous religious orders, which, had they not existed, might have led to a less brutal repression.[171] Take this recent extract from the online Areo magazine.

> Stalin merely tore the existing religious labels off the Christian Inquisition, the enforcement of Christian orthodoxy, the Crusades, the praising of the priesthood, messianism, and Edenic ideas of a terrestrial religious-styled utopia, and re-branded them with the red of communism. Had this Christian machine not been in place, then it is more than likely Stalin wouldn't have had the vehicle he needed to succeed in causing so much suffering in the name of his godless religion, Communism. (Areo magazine: *The Atheist Atrocities Fallacy – Hitler, Stalin and Pol Pot*)[172]

Hitchens, without specifically naming Stalin, concurs:

> Communist absolutists did not so much negate religion, in societies that they well understood were saturated with faith and superstition, as seek to *replace* it. The solemn elevation of infallible leaders who were a source of endless bounty and

---

[171] Stalin is quoted as saying "You know, they are fooling us, there is no God … all this talk about God is sheer nonsense" in E. Yaroslavsky, *Landmarks in the Life of Stalin*, Foreign Languages Publishing House, Moscow 1940.

[172] See the section headed 'Stalin' at *https://areomagazine.com/2017/02/17/the-atheist-atrocities-fallacy-hitler-stalin-and-pol-pot/25*

blessing; the permanent search for heretics and schismatics; the mummification of dead leaders as icon and relics; the lurid show trials that elicited incredible confessions by means of torture ... none of this was very difficult to interpret in traditional terms.[173]

So, religion is not only responsible for abuses inside its own front doors, but also for those who copy its methods in other contexts. The practical difficulty for the proponents of this particular brand of atheism is how they intend to stop the spread of religion. Instigating some sort of ideological policing system is something they themselves would not support. In espousing the need for freedom to think without the shackles of inculcated religious indoctrination, they cannot then themselves impose an embargo on the freedom to exercise religious faith: persuasion is their only option. Hitchens believes humanity can progress through science, reason and philosophy much more than through religion. His inclusion of philosophy is, however, weakened by his subtitle which pre-empts his conclusion. '*How* Religion Poisons Everything' should be '*Does* Religion Poison Everything?' if it is to lay claim to be properly philosophical.

Of course, beliefs and ideologies can be used to justify the infliction of harm and this is the charge Christopher Hitchens brings against religion. How could we test whether Stalin would have been less brutal if he had not inherited a long history of institutional religious abuse? The only way to apply scientific method to this question would be to **rerun history without religion** and examine whether Stalin was indeed as brutal. Hitchens' thesis must remain in the realm of speculation. Another atheist writer, Russell Blackford, takes

---

[173] *god is not Great, How Religion Poisons Everything*, page 246

135

a less acute stance on the role of ideology in totalitarian regimes and religious persecutions.

> The Soviet Union was undeniably an atheist state, and the same applies to Maoist China and to Pol Pot's fanatical Khmer Rouge regime in Cambodia in the 1970s. That does not, however, show that the atrocities committed by these totalitarian dictatorships were the result of atheist beliefs, carried out in the name of atheism, or caused primarily by the atheistic aspects of the relevant forms of communism. In all of these cases, the situation was more complex – as, to be fair, also applies to some of the persecutions and atrocities in which religious movements, organizations, and leaders have been deeply implicated over the centuries.[174]

The picture is a much more complex one than simply attributing motivations to particular ideologies. Milgram's famous study in 1961, where American men between twenty and fifty obeyed orders where they thought they were administering increasingly severe electric shocks to subjects of a psychological experiment, has been criticised for its methodology.[175] However, the study was rerun in 2008 by Dr Jerry Burger, of Santa Clara University and separately by Dr Abigail San for the British Broadcasting Corporation under more stringent conditions and the original findings that ordinary people can carry out actions which are completely opposite to their own values were upheld.[176] Milgram was a Jewish psychologist who set out

---

[174] *50 Great Myths about Atheism*, page 88
[175] See Perry, G, (2014) Psychology Review, Volume 20, No 1, Milgram's Obedience Study revisited.
[176] Please see http://news.bbc.co.uk/1/hi/health/7791278.stm for a summary.

to explore why the Nazis had committed such horrendous atrocities in the Second World War. He discovered that ordinary American citizens were capable of inflicting potentially fatal punishment under instruction. There are variations and questions about some of the reruns, but the overall conclusion is that people, both men and women, act very differently under institutional authority than they do when given genuine freedom of choice. [177] In an interview on a programme called *Sixty Minutes* in 1979, Milgram said this in response to the question, "Are you suggesting that, that it could happen here? "

I would say, on the basis of having observed a thousand people in the experiment and having my own intuition shaped and informed by these experiments, that if a system of death camps were set up in the United States of the sort we had seen in Nazi Germany, one would be able to find sufficient personnel for those camps in any medium-sized American town. (Milgram) [178]

Hitchens' account of the role of religion is at odds with the findings of Milgram's study and for him to justify his assertion that religion is the root cause of acts of genocide, he would need to show that the majority of the subjects in the obedience experiments were religiously motivated. This is potentially open to research, but to the best of my knowledge has not been attempted.

---

[177] Tim Edwards has suggested that a modern equivalent can be found in a widespread acceptance in America of the use of Guantanamo Bay, where the US Government detained terrorist suspects following the 9/11 attacks. This includes, for some, an endorsement of the waterboarding technique.

[178] Please see https://www.azquotes.com/author/10075-Stanley_Milgram where this quote is found.

Belief, Truth and Human Behaviour

> Here is an imaginary scenario to look at whether the truth or falsity of a belief is the key factor determining the behaviour of the people involved.

In order to explore further the notion that human nature is much more than a repressed innocence that will flourish once pernicious ideologies, including religion, are shown to be false, I want to use a hypothetical example. Take the case of a murder. Imagine a man is charged with murder and held on remand. Whilst in custody, he is mistreated and humiliated by the prison guards in front of the other prisoners. His trial is held, and he is rightly found guilty of murder.

Believing that the prisoner is guilty

In the first instance, the prison officers believed that the subject was guilty. Was it this belief which drove them to humiliate the prisoner? The prison guards' belief the prisoner is guilty does not in itself explain why they might humiliate him, because it is perfectly possible to believe he is guilty and treat him with dignity. Even if one particular guard feels justified in using his belief that the prisoner is guilty to humiliate the prisoner, is the second guard equally influenced by the belief of guilt or is it the behaviour of the first guard that influences his own behaviour towards the prisoner? The dynamics of group behaviour also need to be factored in.

Uncertainty about guilt or innocence

Suppose we take away the belief about guilt or innocence, we still find there is an unresolved problem. Imagine a prisoner arrives but it is not known why that particular person has been brought to the prison. Recently there was a case of one particular prisoner who was **mistakenly** convicted of a crime, so the prison guards are even more uncertain about this prisoner's guilt or innocence, and don't even know what he has been charged with. How they treat the prisoner is still an issue even though they have no belief pertaining to his guilt or innocence. Are they subject to the expectations of other guards? Is the Chief Prison Officer someone to be scared of, so the stricter you are with the prisoners the better light you are seen in? Is the connection between our social and institutional relationships and our beliefs subject to individual variation? All these factors and more combine together to create a culture.

The Prisoner is not Guilty

Now consider another case where exactly the same thing happens but on this occasion the subject is rightly found **not** guilty. The prison guards believe in this instance that the prisoner is innocent. This does not mean that whilst on remand the prisoner will have been spared any humiliation. He may have had personality traits the other guards and prisoners may have found irritating and for that reason may have been bullied.

What this entire example shows – and surely it has happened in one form or another many times – is that the truth about the ultimate focal point of an issue is not the sole or even the most significant determinant of the human behaviour associated with that issue. Belief about another person's religion or behaviour can be used as a justification to mistreat and humiliate other people. However, such attitudes can just as easily stem from the need to conform to institutional pressure, group norms or simply the desire to exercise personal power.[179] So how do the complexities of human interaction relate to religious belief? I want to suggest that isolating belief away from other characteristics of human nature is too simplistic an equation from which to draw any substantive conclusion.

Religion and Violence

> What are the causes of religious violence?

Asking whether science is good or bad for human beings is not dissimilar to asking if religion is good or bad for humanity. Take Hertha Ayrton, the scientist who developed a device to blow away poisonous gases from the trenches in World War I. Here, science was the means through which the poisonous gases were manufactured in the first place, but also the means through which the preventive device was developed. It is not science itself that is good or bad; such attributions apply only to how science is used. Why is religion not seen in this way? Why is science understood to be more complex, but religion allowed to be simplified to good or bad? In most examples of the religion/science discourse, science is referred to mainly in the context of research science rather than applied science. It is clear that some scientific knowledge is used destructively, both humanly and environmentally, while other applications respect the environment and enhance the health and wellbeing of animals and human beings.[180]

---

[179] Philip Zimbardo's famous 1971 Stanford Prisoner experiment demonstrated how ambivalent guidance from authority figures can bring about institutional abuse. Michel Foucault wrote extensively as to how people are shaped by historical and cultural influences.

[180] Pinker's list of scientists who have reminded the world about the dangers of nuclear war misses the point because scientists themselves do not control the ways scientific knowledge is used. (See *Enlightenment Now. The Case for Reason, Science and Humanism*, page. 308.)

Likewise, it follows that it is not religious belief itself which is inherently good or bad but what effect it has in its application.[181] Heather Selma Gregg's 2004 dissertation says "bellicose interpretations of religions have accompanied waves of religious violence." [182] She points to Muslim, Hindu, Buddhist, Jewish and Christian examples, but she says,

> All the world's major religions have gone through periods of violence as a means of attaining specific goals ... Islam is not unique in its use of force to achieve saliently religious goals ... this dissertation has argued that none of these religions has been consistently violent; rather, all have gone through periods of bellicosity and periods of peace. This suggests that something within religion changes, making it violent at some points and places but not others. To answer this puzzle, this dissertation has argued that religious violence is the result of *interpretations* of a given faith, which are the product of individuals grounded in specific circumstances. Therefore, religious beliefs, doctrines, scriptures and rituals are not the cause of violence *per se*, but rather specific interpretations, which vary according to individuals, time, and place.[183]

Ideologies and belief systems have a force but there are **vast differences** in the way they are used and interpreted from **within** particular communities. Christopher De Bellaigue illustrates this

---

[181] A famous saying of Christ was "By their fruit you will recognise them", implying that what is done is the real evidence of intention, rather than what is said.

[182] *The Causes of Religious Wars: Holy Nations, Sacred Spaces, and Religious Revolutions* (Unpublished doctoral dissertation) page 468

[183] Ibid, pages 467-8

very point in his book, subtitled 'The Modern Struggle between Faith and Reason'. His conclusion seriously questions whether the radical and liberal ends of the Muslim world really have anything in common with each other at all. He says this in his introduction:

> It suffices to open our eyes to see millions of people of Muslim faith or origin in the Western world who lead lives that have successfully incorporated the modern[184] values of tolerance, empiricism, and the internalisation or dilution of faith ... They do not behead, rampage or try to convert their non-Muslim neighbours.[185]

De Bellaigue goes on to explain that since the First World War a sense of alienation which many Muslims feel from society at large has also been mirrored by an alienation from the traditional roots of Islam itself.

> What, if anything, links these angry, often ill-informed Muslims to the entrepreneurial Iranian Americans who hold Sufi prayer meetings and engage in philanthropy in suburban Los Angeles? ... It is far from certain whether these people belong to the same community or different opposing ones.[186]

It is immediately obvious that just below the surface of any one labelled group are a complex and wide-ranging set of attitudes and inclinations which are very hard to disentangle. A 2013 study by

---

[184] Some may argue such values have a longer inheritance in Islam.
[185] *The Islamic Enlightenment, The Modern Struggle between Faith and Reason,* page xx (Introduction)
[186] Ibid, page 350

Muluk, Sumaktoyo and Ruth in Indonesia showed the greater the devotion to religious practice, the less support there was for violence potentially justified by Islamic law .[187] When discussing the role of religious actors and organisations involved in peacebuilding processes,[188] Svensson points out that "in general, interpretations of religious message conducive to peace making and peacebuilding require a deeper religious interpretation that often goes beyond the superficial literal interpretations in the Holy Scriptures of the religious traditions (that invariably consist of elements that glorify, sanctify, or legitimatize violence, "othering", or intolerance)." [189] On this basis, it is possible to argue that sincere reflective questioning within religious practice is more likely to lead to peacebuilding than incitement to conflict. When faith is relational, then there is much more opportunity, as in the case of the psalmist in the Old Testament or Job when he was struggling to understand the reason for his suffering, for questioning God within the faith relationship, essentially through honest prayer. However, it is difficult to generalise from such studies because there is a variation in charismatic qualities between different leaders in different political settings. So, any assessment of whether a conflict is fuelled and perpetuated by religious zeal or by an underlying political agenda will need to take account of how the religion is being taught to those in the forefront of the conflict.

---

[187] Asian Journal of Social Psychology, Vol.16, No.2,2013 pages 101-111

[188] Svensson points out that to assess the role of religion in conflicts, an assessment of the role of religion in peace-making is also required.

[189] Handbook of Religion and Society,2016, page 479. Example texts regarding peace: 1) Judaism: "God announceth to Jerusalem that they [Israel] will be redeemed only through peace" (Deuteronomy Rabah 5:15). 2) Islam: The Quran further states that if you deal with your enemy positively and return good for evil, he will become your closest friend (41:34). 3) Christianity: "Therefore, being justified by faith, we have peace with God through our Lord Jesus Christ" (Romans 5:1).

In contrast to the Indonesian study, Horowitz in 2009 suggested that conflicts can be prolonged and more difficult to resolve when religious factors are involved; that is, it becomes more difficult to give way when ideological beliefs are used to justify a conflict.[190] Svensson points out that monotheistic tradition can be seen as "particularly exclusive and by its nature more prone to zero-sum ideological battles and, ultimately violence.[191] Although it seems there are periods of peace and periods of conflict in all the major religions, a stark contrast has been drawn by Kang in his paper, "Why was there no religious war in premodern Asia?" However, what his summary reveals is that in premodern East Asia, Korea, Japan, Vietnam, and China, very few of the 950 entries of violence were religious during the 473 year span of the study. The absence of religious violence, however, did not prevent violence *per se*. Svensson cites three studies identifying that rather than religious diversity, it is religious **segregation** and **linguistic differences** that are precipitating factors which increase the risk of conflict, particularly when the religious demographic is affected by **political repression and accommodation**.[192]

Gregg's thesis (page 468) provides a more complicated view of religious wars as fuelled by a combination of factors, namely "threat perception; the prevalence of material, social and technological

---

[190] International Security, Vol.34,No.2, 2009, pages 162-193

[191] Handbook of Religion and Society,2016, page 471. Of the three main monotheistic religions, Christianity is the only one where the relevant scriptures were radically revised by Christ himself. Christ claimed to be the "Messiah" (St. Mark's Gospel 8:29-30), while Muhammed thought himself to be a prophet for the Arabs who had never had one before *Islam, A short History,* page 4. The concept of an Islamic State is a possibility which some Muslims believe has a theological basis; the Holy Land is also theologically woven into Judaism; for Christianity the mission is to "Go into all the world and preach the gospel to all creation" (St. Mark's Gospel 16:15).

[192] Ibid, page 471. The studies referred to are Dowd (2014, 2015), Boreman (2015) and Nordas (2014).

resources; and the relationship between political and religious leaders". It appears that threat perception, combined with a desire to secure territory or recapture Holy Sites, are often triggers for violent religious conflict, coupled with a close alliance with those in power.

In relation to the issue of religion and conflict, it is helpful to try and identify a conflict with which one might be culturally familiar. The violent conflict in Northern Ireland stretched from 1968 to the Good Friday Agreement in 1998. Rhetorically speaking, in order to show how difficult it is to separate the religious, political and cultural dimensions, we can ask ourselves what the causes were. Simply reflecting on the question poses the problem as to what methodologies are most appropriate for discovering if the fundamental issues were religious, political or cultural, or a mixture of all three. Should the latter be the case, as one might suspect, how can a proportion be properly ascribed to each?

Love and Judgement

> Our inclination rails against the idea of hell: is it an insidious distraction from the proper use of our intelligence? What is the Christian teaching about judging others?

In his lecture on why he was not a Christian, Russell captured the deep reservations that many people, including Christians, have about the way the concept of hell is used in churches and religious education. He was critical of Christ himself for threatening eternal punishment for those who would not accept his preaching. Understandably, there is an antipathy towards using fear as a tool to drive people towards faith in God. Russell's view is that intelligence should and will overcome superstition. He felt that belief in God was a backdoor way of not facing up to the realities of life and relinquishing a true independence of mind.

Intelligence falls exactly into the same category as religion and science. It is not about how much intelligence we have, it is about how we use it. Modern understanding of hell is confined to the "living hells" that humans have perpetrated on one another, irrespective of whether or not they are aligned to religious or other beliefs or to non-believers. The extreme examples of death camps, displacement, lack of medical care, criminal brutality and gangland style revenge are all around for us to see and distance ourselves from, perhaps in the temporary comfort of an armchair. These human acts of cruelty can have the effect of inflicting "eternal" separation between loved ones. In *Anne Frank – In the Secret Annexe*, we read this: "After their deportation to Auschwitz-Birkenau, the men and women are separated for good … It's a well organised hell." [193]

Whereas Christians wrestle with what hell actually means, atheists on the other hand already accept that death is permanent separation from everything; the deeper implication is that the experiences they have of love, trust and compassion, precious though they are, have no other source than flawed human beings. This glimpse into "paradise" may of course increase the perceived value of such experiences, simply because of their transient nature. Atheists accommodate the idea of permanent and irretrievable separation within their own philosophical outlook, so they may not be as far away from the idea of a final state of oblivion as their condemnation of the concept of hell suggests. Perhaps death is easier to comprehend in a context where nothing can last forever.

So how is "hell" viewed by Christians? One view is that Christ was reacting to the increasing pressure he was under as a human being as

---

[193]   *Anne Frank – In the Secret Annexe*, page 46

he knowingly approached his own death as well as his awareness of what his death meant for the human race. Another approach is that Christ genuinely felt people can reach a moral and spiritual point of no return, an irretrievable breakdown in their relationship with God. Nevertheless, terrifying as the prospect of hell is, the application of human criteria to God's judgement must always be flawed.

Much of Christ's teaching was about the moral and spiritual choices people face. There is a strong element of poor choices bringing their own cost or 'punishment', an ultimate lack of purpose and fulfilment, with them. However, there was also a very strong, if under-reported, aspect of his teaching, emphasising that human beings are *not* asked to exercise judgement on God's behalf. An often-quoted text from St Mathew's Gospel as proof that Christianity is punitive is:

> When the Son of Man comes in his glory, and all the angels with him, he will sit on his throne in heavenly glory. All the nations will be gathered before him, and he will separate the people one from another, as a shepherd separates the sheep from the goats. (St Matthew's Gospel 25:31-33)

The preceding text, however, warns against prejudging other people through human eyes. Those who preach hell and damnation should always be aware it is they who may end up being the goats. Many Christians do not see it as their role to judge others, but only to trust in a God who says loving others is the ultimate way to heal, rather than seek revenge.[194] It is not, however, fearmongering to talk about the cost of actions and attitudes which break down

---

[194] Likewise, for huge numbers of Muslims the imposition of an Islamic state is not the goal. Rather, the aim is to fulfil religious duties to the benefit of others and of Allah.

relationships rather than enhance them, like the film of 'Sophie's Choice,' where the cost can sometimes be final. Of course, in order to even attempt such an approach to faith where forgiveness is more to do with healing the spirit than self-obsessed martyrdom, an inner strength is needed, and so belief in Christ as God is justified as an active part of finding that strength. Underlying this is the sense that a limited and fractured view of love and attachment means a more perfect experience is possible.[195] For many, this is the substance of faith rather than simply the promise of a satisfying after-life.

Conclusion

> Is human nature just shackled by religion or is there a deeper problem?

Critiques such as Russell's point to some of the dilemmas Christians face about the character of God, but the repudiation he makes of religious belief is counterbalanced by his vision of how to make the world a better place. He believes the world needs kindliness and courage, and his fundamental solution is to promote the flourishing of an unshackled and fearless use of our ability to think.

What can we deduce about Russell's vision of progress? It assumes an increase in knowledge is the key to creating a better future. If this

---

[195] Not everyone has the *same* inner sense. Christopher Hitchens called his old religious knowledge teacher a "pious old trout" after she had said God made vegetation green because it was more restful to our eyes. He said at the age of nine he had no conception of the relationship between photosynthesis and chlorophyll but "simply knew, almost as if I had privileged access to a higher authority, that my teacher had managed to get everything wrong in just two sentences. The eyes were adjusted to nature, and not the other way about" (*god is not Great*, pages 2-3). Even atheists can experience an inner sense of what they believe to be true without concrete factual evidence to back it up.

is to be the case, then it also must be true that our cognitive capacities are more powerful than our instincts for self-preservation through defensive or aggressive means. It also must be true that the more we learn, the more likely we are to develop kindliness and courage. The process of self-discovery gives us a sense of control which enhances positive moral qualities, even though we know there is no frame of reference beyond our own existence. Russell's view of human nature is based on the idea of a 'rational' plateau being uncovered following the removal of old prejudices. It is as if Russell is saying that once we have freed ourselves from the shackles of religion, that hard-won freedom will allow us an unfettered path to improve the world.

The prisoner example in the preceding section hopefully showed that the human predicament is much deeper than simply removing false ideologies to reveal a previously repressed innocence. Russell's conception of the power of intelligence can be used for the good, neglect or even harm of others. Genuine though thinkers like Russell are, it is impossible to carve out a 'value free' zone in which the most intelligent can persuade everyone else what is best for humanity.[196] The fundamental problem is that no one, including academics and philosophers, can exempt themselves from self-interest.

We do not shut down all prisons because abuse takes place in some, we don't make churches illegal because abuse has occurred within some, and we don't shut down scientific activity because some scientific knowledge is used for harm. We are thinking, moral, animal, confused, social and self-preserving creatures. Something more than cognitive remodelling is required. The attraction of faith, despite its incongruities, is that it uses both internal and external resources. Is it contrary to modern interpretations of the Enlightenment? I will discuss this question in the next chapter, examining the claim that

---

[196] We would also have to agree what intelligence consisted of.

reason is the main way we can develop a better world. Russell's hopes have a resonance with the post Second World War aspiration that rationality would rule after the horrors of the conflict. One only has to name examples such as Vietnam, Cambodia, Rwanda/Burundi, the Democratic Republic of Congo, South Africa, the former Yugoslavia, Iraq, the Middle East and Yemen, and there are so many others, to show that the human predicament remains unsolved.

Chapter 9
The New Enlightenment Project

A Confession

> Are people who hold faith beliefs devoid of reason?

I have read much atheist writing in the development of this piece, particularly about the way the faith community is viewed in the 21st century by Enlightenment thinkers. At the extreme, those who practise faith are characterised as deluded, unthinking, emotionally dependant, willing to use fear to subdue others and, perhaps most of all, intolerant. Stephen Pinker, the champion of what is known as The New Enlightenment Project, says:

> If there's anything the Enlightenment thinkers had in common, it was an insistence that we energetically apply the standard of reasoning to understand our world, and not fall back on generators of delusion like faith, dogma, revelation, authority, charisma, mysticism, divination, visions, gut feelings, or the hermeneutic parsing of sacred texts.[197]

---

[197]   *Enlightenment Now. The Case for Reason, Science and Humanism*, page 8

This is now the moment to say that I am a practising Christian. I will say more later. I am as vulnerable to weaknesses as anyone else, but I don't recognise myself as someone who negates reason;[198] neither would I describe the vast majority of people I have known who practise faith, including some who practice other faiths and come from other cultures, in the same way.[199]

Reason is the Key to Progress

> Can we shed all the influences in us and on us and just use reason to solve problems?

Stephen Pinker describes a technique used by rabbis in the past to improve reasoning in the context of making the world 'more rational'. The rabbis compelled their students to argue a case from the other side of a Talmudic debate. He adds a modern application where those on different sides of a conflict are made to set up empirical tests which are used to settle the issue at stake.[200] I have, as best I can, tried to use my interest in philosophy to see the issues from other points of view to my own as I have written the preceding chapters.

The issue here is whether it is reasonable to rely on reason *alone* to arrive at a way of understanding the world; does such sole reliance address the full extent of human experience? I hope some of the earlier sections on relational knowledge, i.e. our experience of knowing other people, indicate that this form of knowledge should

---

[198] Of course, I may be deluded about that.

[199] I was born into the Parsee culture, which emanates from Mumbai; the religion practised is Zoroastrianism.

[200] *Enlightenment Now. The Case for Reason, Science and Humanism*, page 379. The method referred to is called 'Adversarial Collaboration': Mellars, Hertwig Kahneman, 2001.

not be discounted simply because it is much harder to analyse through traditional empirical scientific methods. Our minds and our feelings need to be in some kind of relative harmony with each other for us to *think* and *feel* about the world in a coherent way.

According to Pinker, those who are best at predicting human behaviour exhibit particular traits which amount to them being less driven by the bias of their own tribe, faith or political allegiance compared to others. The appropriate qualities are intellectual curiosity, a taste for variety, pleasure taken in intellectual activity, appreciating uncertainty and seeing multiple sides of an issue.[201] They are some of the qualities of a very good civil servant. The best predictors appear to be those who refrain from adopting fixed positions. It is of course a prerequisite of such an approach that the social situation of the predictor is relatively free from undue pressure from other people or institutions to think and act without fear of any consequence that might have adverse implications for them. This of course does not imply that those same people also enjoy the most fulfilled relationships or have the greatest courage when faced with adversity.

Pinker describes the changes which figures like Galileo, Newton and Laplace brought about in our global thinking. We were now no longer subjects of a "cosmic morality play" in which the "universe is saturated with purpose", wherein everything that goes wrong is always someone's fault, human, divine or satanic.[202] Pinker qualifies this by saying that "*People* have goals, of course, but projecting goals onto the workings of nature is an illusion. Things can happen without anyone taking into account their effects on human happiness."

---

[201] *Enlightenment Now. The Case for Reason, Science and Humanism*, page 369
[202] Ibid, page 24

(emphasis original)[203] For Pinker, the world is a combination of disorder, evolutionary forces and information, the latter being the brain's capacity to absorb and use information intelligently. Against these forces, the sympathy we feel for others combined with reason and based on the model science has given us can make the world a slightly better place. Pinker aligns himself with Hans Rosling, who said, "I am not an optimist. I'm a very serious possibilist." [204] We are in a state of tension between the forces of disorder and the more positive forces promoted by the Enlightenment.

Pinker places reason into a context which reveals the uphill struggle it faces. Take the example of poverty, which he describes in two ways: "poverty, too, needs no explanation. In a world governed by entropy and evolution, it is the default state of humankind." [205] He says, "seven hundred million people in the world today live in extreme poverty. In the regions where they are concentrated, life expectancy is less than 60, and almost a quarter of the people are undernourished." [206] In contrast, he then says, "the world is about a hundred times wealthier today than it was two centuries ago, and the prosperity is becoming more evenly distributed across the world's countries and people." [207] He gives both negative and positive ways of describing poverty in an attempt to capture what he believes is the same story. The way a story is told can easily affect how a problem

---

[203] Ibid, page 203. It could easily follow that it is also a mistake to think human agency can be explained by projecting the workings of nature onto it. This does not suit Pinker's evolutionary stance, and in any event, the mind-body debate as discussed in Chapter 2 suggests that to represent human decision making in terms of predetermined mechanics is not the direction that researchers are pursuing. Their goal is to work on the interaction between parts of the brain and to uncover the neurological conditions in which decisions can be made.

[204] Ibid, page 345

[205] Ibid, page 25

[206] Ibid, page 325

[207] Ibid, page 322

is perceived. His assertion is that when a historical 'helicopter' view is taken on major issues world-wide, things *are* improving, despite setbacks.

Pinker's basic tools are taken from the social sciences and they focus on measurement, that is, the measurement of human experience, security, wealth, health, peace and several other factors. This is what he primarily means by abandoning "generators of delusion" and using empirical methods as the chief means of improving the human condition.[208] However, he never defines reason in technical terms.

Imagination, Religion and Relationships

Does imagination in art and religion have a more significant history than we realise?

Pinker might agree with John Broome by saying that in reasoning, "you operate on the contents of your premise attitudes to construct the content of your conclusion attitude." [209] However, the reality of reasoning is not as smooth as the theory would have us believe. John Broome goes on to use the example of a mathematician formulating a theory:

Take a mathematician's thinking, for example. A mathematician might start a project by forming a plausible conjecture. That is not reasoning. Then she might go on to try and piece together a proof of the conjecture. No doubt there will be a lot of reasoning in the course of doing that ... But she will also do a lot of thinking that is not reasoning: she will choose which line

---

208 Ibid, page 8
209 *Rationality Through Reasoning*, page 231

of research to follow, she might be inspired by a sudden idea to try a particular move, or she might visualize the problem geometrically. Often in practice she will come to believe the conclusion earlier in her thinking process.[210]

The point at issue is that reasoning is not 'detachable' from other influences – imagination, impulse and accidental discovery are in reality all part of the process. In fact, the role of myth and 'supernatural' belief systems as part of human functioning were essential ingredients in the rise of Homo Sapiens, according to Yuval Noah Harari. Religion, commerce, social stratification have been tied up with each other since the emergence of our species, as he suggests in the following passage:

> The period from about 70,000 years ago to about 30,000 years ago witnessed the invention of boats, oil lamps, bows and arrows and needles (essential for sewing warm clothing). The first objects that can reliably be called art date from this era … as does the first clear evidence for religion, commerce and social stratification.[211]

Harari's theory is that it *is* precisely the human capacity for imagination and myth which is inextricably linked to the cognitive revolution which led to the domination of the earth by us, Homo Sapiens. From Pinker's perspective, what was an adaptive advantage 70,000 years ago is now a redundant appendage.[212] How easily is

---

[210] Ibid, pages 244-5
[211] *Sapiens*, page 23
[212] He accepts the current use of religious culture provided there is no actual belief in a Godhead.

religious belief shaken off? Karen Armstrong has this to say about the intertwining of imagination and religion:

> Religious people are trained to look beneath the unpromising surface to find the sacred within it. They have to use their creative imaginations. Jean-Paul Sartre defined the imagination as the ability to think of what is not present. Human beings are religious creatures because they are imaginative; they are so constituted that they are compelled to search for hidden meaning and to achieve an ecstasy that makes them feel fully alive.[213]

If religion and imagination are inextricably linked, and that combination is central to human cognitive development, Pinker is suggesting that we drop "faith, dogma, revelation, authority, charisma, mysticism, divination, visions, gut feelings, or the hermeneutic parsing of sacred texts" but hold on to our imagination.[214] Imagine you are unfortunate enough to be in a marriage which is not working. As you privately contemplate divorce, the effect it might have on your children, the consequences for everyone, including your partner, how easily are you able to disregard what Pinker calls "gut feelings" and focus only on what reason tells you to do? [215] In deciding my course of action, do I take everyone's feelings into account even if they are not fully grounded? For example, one of my children is terrified that he will not see me if I leave, even though I am promising to see him regularly. Should I ignore those feelings because I believe they are ill-founded? I think my wife's feelings are biased and she is feeding my

---

[213] *Islam, A Short History*, page x (Introduction)
[214] *Enlightenment Now. The Case for Reason, Science and Humanism*, page 8
[215] *Enlightenment Now. The Case for Reason, Science and Humanism*, page 8

son's fears. Shall I just focus on what everyone should be thinking, and discount their 'irrational' fears?

I hope this illustration shows how impossible it is to implement Pinker's approach to reason in difficult relational issues; it also shows how the interpretation of what is 'reason' and what is 'bias' is not incontrovertible. To ignore 'gut feelings' is not to disregard all other considerations; to discard them entirely could be seen as unreasonable in itself. It is not uncommon to puzzle over what the hidden feelings in such a situation are. It is perfectly possible to use the idea of 'reason' to unfairly exert power over others by dismissing their feelings as 'irrational'. There is more than one reasonable solution to a problem. This is why Broome says that "our intuitive idea of correctness does not even rule out the possibility that there may be more than one correct way to reason on the basis of some particular premise attitudes." [216] Pinker's view of reason is a legitimate one, but he focuses on policy making, institutions and democratic practice. It is not a view of reason that easily translates across the whole spectrum of human experience, valuable though it might be in the analysis of government policy, education and other public endeavours. When we are under pressure, we do not take comfort from statistical averages.

Reason without Feeling

What happens when we can reason but cannot feel? Do reason and feeling depend on each other for there to be successful relationships?

---

[216] *Rationality Through Reasoning*, page 247

The following thought experiment may help to clarify the point. The thought experiment is as follows: imagine that the existence of God,[217] both personal and creative, is mathematically proven, but we are not given any additional information apart from the way the natural and biological world is at present. The question is, 'How exactly would that discovery affect atheistic thinking?' As long as there was no divine intervention in human affairs, it is very hard to see what impact such a proof would make. The key point, I believe, is that it would **not change** the human predicament, however we define it; it would neither change how we related to one another or used the resources of the natural world. To know there was a God without knowing anything about the character of God would leave us none the wiser. It would, to put it bluntly, make **no difference** whether God existed or not. Reason alone does not address the full range of human needs, which include the emotional, spiritual, social and cognitive, so it makes sense that mathematics alone cannot fully impact on the human condition.

It was Domasio's study, quoted in Chapter 2, which revealed the chasm between theoretical and relational understanding in studies where brain damage to areas responsible for emotional functioning has occurred. I want to briefly remind you of the key message: "these patients exhibit extensive knowledge about the social situations they so egregiously mismanaged in reality." [218] I want to emphasise again the importance of the link between feeling and thinking through

---

[217] When Stephen Hawking says, "If we find the answer to that" – a complete theory of the universe or universes – "it would be the ultimate triumph of human reason – for then we would know the mind of God", he is not referring to a God who interacts with human beings (*A Brief History of Time*, page 210). He is really saying that we would know all there is to know about the physics of the natural world.

[218] *Looking For Spinoza, Joy, Sorrow and the Feeling Brain*, pages 143-4

his study of patients with specific types of neurological damage. Hume's claim that all our thinking stems from the sensations we experience suggests the mind is captive and has no autonomy of its own. Domasio's work shows, by contrast, the nature of the interdependence of cognition and emotion in the context of our relationships. Hume's position about the subjection of cognitive functioning to the passions is overstated if the expansion of scientific knowledge about the natural world is taken into account, but he was surely right about the impossibility of dissolving the bond between reason and feeling. The connection between mind and feeling was one also made by Christ.

> Hearing that Jesus had silenced the Sadducees, the Pharisees got together. One of them, an expert in the law, tested him with this question: 'Teacher, which is the greatest commandment in the Law?' Jesus replied: 'Love the Lord your God with all your heart and with all your soul and with all your mind.' This is the first and greatest commandment. And the second is like it: 'Love your neighbour as yourself.' All the Law and the Prophets hang on these two commandments. (St. Matthew's Gospel 22:34-40)

It is noteworthy that 'loving one's neighbour' also has to be carried out with heart, soul and mind. Christ and Domasio, with Hume's support, seem a strange combination: where Domasio and Hume depart from Christ is in relation to the latter's belief that God existed at all and further that He himself was God incarnate.

Reason and Faith – an Evolutionary Twist

> We can now redesign parts of nature. What are the implications for the theory of evolution?

As Harari points out, we are now in the unique position of being able to compare the natural world with the biological creations of human beings.

> Today, ... natural selection is facing a completely different challenge ... scientists are engineering living beings. They break the laws of natural selection with impunity ... Eduardo Kac, a Brazilian bio-artist, decided to create a new work of art, a fluorescent green rabbit. Kac contacted a French laboratory ... The French scientists took a run of the mill white rabbit embryo, implanted in its DNA a gene taken from a green fluorescent jellyfish, and *voila!* ... Kac named the rabbit Alba. It is impossible to explain the existence of Alba through the laws of natural selection. She is the product of intelligent design.[219]

Harari gives many other examples in his chapter, entitled 'The End of Homo Sapiens', to support his general contention. What this plethora of astonishing examples of artificial selection uncovers is that we have the potential to radically, rather than cosmetically, design the natural world from the raw materials we have. What is also pertinent is that if the raw materials of nature are so malleable and open to design by ourselves, how can we be so certain there is no intelligence behind the raw materials in the first place? As I previously suggested in Chapter 3, the question of whether there is intelligence behind life should be an open rather than a closed question.

---

[219] *Sapiens*, page 447

The theory of evolution is said to have **proven** that there was no intelligence behind the emergence of life in the first place. Understanding the processes in genetics has given us the capacity to manipulate them. That ability to manipulate them of itself **by implication** reveals a possibility that there is intelligence behind their existence in the first place. If this is ruled out, the only alternative is to say that nature was an accident but our manipulation of it is intentional. We cannot conclusively make that assertion unless we know **everything**, so it necessarily follows that the evidence of evolution is not sufficient proof that there is no God. This point is also acknowledged by Marcus du Sautoy, Professor of Mathematics at Oxford University, who at the same time as rejecting the notion of a "supernatural intelligence that intervenes in the evolution of the universe" [220] says:

> I wonder, though, whether, as I come to the end of my exploration at the limits of knowledge, I have changed my mind about declaring myself an atheist. With my definition of God as the existence of things we cannot know, to declare myself an atheist would mean that I believe there is nothing we cannot know. I don't believe that anymore. [221]

The account of how evolution has replaced God's finger in various aspects of nature is valid in displacing many aspects of creationist theology, but it does not tell us whether there is intelligence behind

---

[220] *What We Cannot Know,* page 411

[221] Ibid, page 411. It is important to note that du Sautoy is not conceding that traditional views of the Deity are in any way correct. For him, God is simply that which we cannot know. He rejects the idea of a God which "people assign strange properties to – such as compassion, wisdom, love – which makes no sense when it comes to the idea that I am exploring" (page 411).

the natural world. Just as in science false assertions can be made, so they can in theology. False assertions in science do not imply that science itself is a fraud any more than false assertions about God prove in themselves that God does not exist.

Human relationships include scientific collaborations and in those relationships the intertwining of reason and feeling is essential for scientific knowledge to progress and grow. For Alba, the *process* involved French scientists, a rabbit embryo and a gene from a jellyfish. However, the intentionality behind the idea came from Kac. Imagine in 20,000 years a researcher might trace the processes in the laboratory involving the scientists, embryo and genetic material. Simply uncovering the genetic trail would not give them the whole story. Could they use research into genetic processes to uncover the relationship between Kac and the French scientists? To discover that, they would need to find evidence of the communication *between* Kac and the scientists, and for that they would need a totally different research method. They would need evidence of communication, but they would also need to understand the *meaning* inherent in the interaction between Kac and the scientists. If all they could find was some fragment of correspondence, they might conclude the fragment was a later addition to augment the story. Of course, that should not be discounted as a possibility, but a possibility is all it could be.

Moral Indignation About Religion

> Where does the moral indignation about religion stem from? What did Christ have to say about it?

There is a great deal of moral outrage from some sources about the damage religion has caused and does cause. The real conundrum is why there should be a sense of outrage about any issue. In a disordered universe, what place does moral outrage fill and what purpose does it serve? Moral outrage surely can only be an optional addition rather than a substantive foundation of life.

Nevertheless, it is surely a misplaced accusation of those who practise religion to accuse non-believers as lacking any basis for the conscience and the moral values they espouse. From a Christian point of view, if humans are made in God's image, they are bound to experience a sense of moral purpose, whether or not they believe in God. Neither is it worth arguing that Christians, for example, do not have disputes about what is right or wrong in certain situations; abortion, sexuality and capital punishment are three issues about which many Christians disagree.

So, there is *no* suggestion that only religious belief can engender true moral behaviour, nor can it absolve believers of having to interpret and work out what for them is right in particular situations. The objection is that if the source of morality is simply evolutionary or a matter of social cooperation, its ultimate value can only be classed as being of an 'intermediate' value. Blackford and Schuklenk, two atheistic writers, acknowledge Haught's point that "a blind, indifferent and amoral natural process, which is how Dawkins has always characterised evolution, can hardly explain why justice, love and the pursuit of truth are now unconditionally binding values." [222]

So even though believers have a more direct argument to make about the source of morality than atheists, a constant criticism atheists make is in relation to the abuse and hypocrisy carried out in the name of religion. Surely if Christ was God incarnate, He would have been able to see the damage religion causes. There can be no doubt Christ Himself was fully aware of religious hypocrisy and abuse carried out in its name.

---

[222] *50 Great Myths about Atheism*, page 71

Now then, you Pharisees clean the outside of the cup and dish, but inside you are full of greed and wickedness … Woe to you Pharisees, because you give God a tenth of your mint, rue and all other kinds of garden herbs, but you neglect justice and the love of God. You should have practised the latter, without leaving the former undone … And you experts in the law, woe to you, because you load people down with burdens they can hardly carry and you yourselves will not lift one finger to help them. (St. Luke's Gospel 11:39, 42, 46)

In fact, Christ went on to say when talking to a very large crowd, "Be on your guard against the yeast of the Pharisees, which is *hypocrisy*" (St. Luke's Gospel 12:1, my emphasis). He went on to tell them about the consequences. "I tell you, my friends, do not be afraid of those who kill the body but after that can do no more. But I will show you whom you should fear. Fear him who after the killing of the body, has power to throw you into hell" (St. Luke's Gospel 12:4-5). It is clear from this and other passages that Christ was fully aware of the destructive effects of corrupt religious practice and its continuing presence in society.

The atheist charge that religion is a prime cause of abuse and hypocrisy was not acceded to by Christ. His view was that religion could be used for selfish and cruel ends, but the human predicament was not simply a case of disorientation, which a large scale Cognitive Behavioural Therapy Programme might fix, i.e. the gradual removal of religious belief from everyday life. It was a more complicated and deeper problem. What is incontrovertible is that Christ himself was fully aware of religious hypocrisy and opposed it ferociously: it is that ferocity which, at least in human terms, led to his death at the hands of Pontius Pilate, egged on by the very Pharisees he challenged.

A Personal Note

In this section I talk a little about my own faith.

I want to quote part of a sermon given at the church I attend by the Vicar, Sandy Christie, on the 20th May 2018, Pentecost Sunday. It is taken from a transcript he has kindly provided. I think it is important to say that the sermon was delivered quietly and calmly. It is a church which seeks to welcome and include both believers and doubters.

But God also breaks in, comes down in another way. By his Spirit. When we put our faith in Jesus, the Spirit comes to rest on us, to dwell within us. What he does is to make God's love in Christ real to our hearts. By his Spirit says Paul, we cry Abba, Father. We know God as our Father. That intimate secure relationship with God becomes a fiery reality in our hearts, not just something we know in our heads. Thomas Goodwin, a 17th century Puritan, explained it like this. He saw a father and son walking together down the street, and suddenly the father took his son and swept him into his arms and hugged him. And then he put him down again and kept walking. Goodwin said – was he any more of a son in his arms than on the street? Legally, objectively, there was no difference. *But experientially, subjectively, there was all the difference in the world.* Children need to be hugged, don't they? When the Holy Spirit comes we know God's love much more deeply in our heart. And that changes us. I am not so worried about what people think of me, or anxious about money, or desperate for that promotion. The Spirit gives me a joyful fearlessness. All that other stuff from the world around doesn't control me anymore. *So we need both the intellectual knowledge of the facts about Jesus – he is where God came down to us. But we also need the experiential reality of the Spirit's assurance that God's love for me in Christ is real, and nothing can separate me from his love. That balance between mind and heart is what we're looking for in authentic church.* Not cold cognitive rationalism – it's not all about 45-minute sermons[223] – or constantly psyching you up to emotional highs. We need both clear teaching about Jesus, and genuine experience of spiritual reality in our hearts. In Acts 2 Peter preaches a long sermon explaining the facts about Jesus. Then at the end it says they were cut to the heart and said what shall we do? *So it is both mind and heart.*[224]

The reason I have quoted this passage, in the context of my argument, is because it talks about the fusion of heart and mind in a way that I can identify with. I have highlighted some sentences which particularly apply in the context of this book. It is important to remember that there are times when I have doubted if I am known by God or when the pressures and injustices of life seem to overwhelm me. Faith is relational; it is based on opening oneself to God without a mathematical proof that He is there. A poem by my friend Tim Edwards includes this line, "We make the bridge by stepping into space."

Without the feeling that Christ Himself was more than a wise man, all of this makes no sense and is little more than a longing for a greater moral and spiritual maturity than I could ever possess. It is that longing which over the years has led me to express an inner

---

[223] Sermons in church rarely exceed 20 minutes.
[224] The title of the sermon was 'Authentic Church'.

hope and as time has gone on, trust in Christ. For that to sustain itself over time, I have had to consider how strong the case is for the claims Christ made about Himself, particularly the significance of the crucifixion and resurrection. I have no answer as to why some unavoidable suffering prevails and if I am honest, I feel that to provide any sort of 'answer' in some way detracts from the gravity of the suffering itself. When Christ on the cross said, "My God, my God why have you forsaken me?" there was no immediate answer (St. Mark's Gospel 15:34). It is rather that Christ came to suffer with us in this life that touches my deeper sense.

To return to the discussion itself, at the end of Chapter 7, I gave a brief summary of where the debate concerning transcendence had reached. I went on to explore if evolution was robust enough to carry the weight of most, if not all, other theories under its wings and concluded that it was not. In this chapter, the idea of reason creating a counterbalance to the impersonal forces of evolution has not succeeded due to the anaesthetising of human experiences into social trends.

Before going on to the two-part conclusion of the book, I want to offer a brief explanation of the rationale for the 3 Appendices, all of which have connections with this particular chapter. Appendix 1 is a brief example of how matters can be pre-judged as 'myth' rather than being 'open to reason'. The idea of resurrection is contrasted with a regular occurrence in the natural world and to an extraordinary incident in the life of a young child in Canada in 2001.

There has been a great deal in this book about reason, feeling and a general sense that one cannot do without the other for a fulfilling life. It has not been within the scope of the book to explore in depth how both reason and feeling might be brought together in harmony. In this chapter, I referred to the two great commandments through which Christ summed up the law. Both commandments are principles to follow and so rational powers are needed to apply them to the ins and outs of our lives, personally, culturally and politically. For this, a proper sense of moral sensibility must **integrate** into life rather than **impose** itself without reference to other influences. Appendix 2 explores this idea in brief.

The discussion about moral outrage in this chapter looked at the issue from the standpoint of why anything should matter if the world was formed from a chaotic and impersonal beginning. However, as you will know, I don't share that view and so think it is important for anyone who professes faith to acknowledge and accept how it has been misused. Appendix 3 gives some examples of this in a Christian context. I cite these examples not to minimize their impact, but to show how difficult it is to live a life of faith without letting it fall foul to institutional and political forces.

Chapter 10
Conclusion (1) – Spaces for Faith in Science

Are there spaces in modern cultures for faith which are compatible with the march of science?

The title 'Spaces for Faith' may seem strangely apologetic in its defence of the credibility of faith: modern secular culture, despite its interface with multiculturalism, is crowded with competing explanations of how we should see the natural world, most of which discard the idea of a creative intelligence as an anachronistic comfort blanket. So, in the context of an overriding blast of cynicism about faith in a personal God, 'spaces' provides the appropriate register for the sceptical mind. There are two spaces I will explore here in Chapter 10: firstly, entropy and our perception of time and secondly, the separation of fact and myth. In Chapter 11, I will discuss the forward direction of the human race and where we see ourselves in relation to the knowledge we hold.

Why are these 'spaces' relevant to the prospect of faith? Whether you call human agency and its consequences for society moral or political, there is a clear understanding emerging from within atheist writings that the nature of the choices human beings make individually and communally have a vital significance. I start with the question of the objectivity of scientific knowledge.

Entropy and Our Perception of Time

How does time fit in with our understanding of the fundamentals of life?

I want to suggest that any claim suggesting the theory of evolution is the final frontier of knowledge is compromised by the emergence of quantum theory: in quantum theory, 'time' is an *internal* species of perception rather than an objective framework into which reality fits. However, Carlo Rovelli in *The Order of Time* says, "A minimum interval of time exists. Below this, the notion of time does not exist – even in its most basic meaning." [225] This means that we do not examine the natural world as placed within the framework of time and space in the way the theory of evolution does, but rather see both time and space as being moveable factors inside an intriguing 'web' of reality: they are not *externally fixed frameworks* for everything else. Time and space don't have a permanent status in the natural world, even though our own senses tell us otherwise.

As time and space are variables, there are, additionally in quantum theory, situations where time and space do not exist *at all*. There are 'black hole' situations which are so compressed that nothing in them can be measured, including light and heat as well as space and time. I am definitely not a scientist, but famous physicists have attempted in recent times to convey their research to the layperson; I am attempting to interpret some of the content in terms of whether we are inside or outside of the observation process. Essentially, our capacity for observation is *internal* to our perception of time – there is a world beyond where time might slow down or quicken or not be there at

---

[225] *The Order of Time*, pages 74-5. Rovelli is referring to the 'Planck' scale of time

all. Professor Kip Thorne, in the introduction to Stephen Hawking's final book, *Brief Answers to the Big Questions*, says this: "Because gravitational waves are a form of space warp they are produced most strongly by objects that themselves are made wholly or partially from warped space-time - which means, especially, by black holes." [226]

It seems very hard to imagine a clock where the speed of 'one second' slows down or quickens, but that is what we are talking about. There is no **absolute** standard of 'one second' – its actual duration varies according to the strength or weakness of the 'pull' of nearby gravitational forces.

One circumstance, however, where time **has** to be part of the natural world, is entropy. Entropy is the frequency of molecular movement which is specifically related to changes in temperature. Carlo Rovelli puts it in this way:

The entropy of the world in the far past appears very low to us. But this might not reflect the exact state of the world: it might regard the subset of the world's variables with which *we*, as physical systems have interacted.[227]

The implication of this inference is clear.

We observe the universe from within it … It measures something that relates to us more than the cosmos.[228]

What Rovelli goes on to say is that it is possible our sense of time is a product of only those situations where interaction has taken

---

[226] *Brief Answers to the Big Questions*, pages xviii-xix
[227] *The Order of Time*, page 128
[228] Ibid, page 134

place with the parts of the universe that have low rates of molecular movement: "With regard to *these* systems, entropy is constantly increasing. There, and not elsewhere, there are the typical phenomena associated with the flowing of time: life is possible, together with evolution, thought and our awareness of time passing." [229] The basis of evolution from this perspective is that the natural world has grown out of the increasing disorder or entropy of the basic elements in the cosmos so the random genetic mutations which *do* manage to connect with environmental advantages have a greater chance of reoccurring: there is a greater chance of this happening with an increasing range of alternative possibilities or, to put it another way, an increasing amount of molecular disorder.

Our evolutionary perspective is only part of the explanation of the natural world: for example, oxygen and water exist both *within* us and *beyond* ourselves. Our bodies contain electromagnetic forces, and such forces exist in the wider universe and did so before organic life as we know it appeared. At the most fundamental levels we have reached in our observation techniques, we have realised that our interaction in the process necessarily *limits* what there is to see. From those limited observations where there is low entropy, more complex systems have emerged and those systems that depend on time, such as reproduction in evolutionary history, are built on those fundamentals.

There are 'innumerable variables' with which we are not interacting. The circumstances of increasing complexity which we observe include our life and being, but not the whole of the cosmos. Entropy in this respect only applies to the parts of the cosmos *we* interact with through observation. Stephen Hawking in *Brief Answers to the Big Questions* makes the same point in an entirely

---

[229] Ibid, page 131

different way: "Thus the very fact that we exist as beings that can ask the question 'Why is the universe the way it is?' is a restriction on the history we live in. It implies it is one of the minority of histories that have galaxies and stars." [230] Hawking himself prefers a theory that can relate other universes to what we already know about our universe, because to accept the alternative would imply that what we don't know will **always** remain unknowable. We would always be in a fog of ignorance about 'elsewhere' no matter how much we had discovered about our own world.

Evolution as presented by both Rovelli and Hawking is in fact a subset of something much greater and much more mysterious. It is not a theory that explains all. Evolutionary biology cannot explain quantum activity, but quantum activity is inextricably linked to organic life and therefore evolution.

Problematically, this 'greater' picture of quantum theories is shrouded in mystery. It is a world that combines uncertainty with predictions, and one where particles appear when interacting with others but disappear when not. Observations limit outcomes but a much wider range of possibilities exist when no such observations occur. It is a world where endless possibilities occur within a finite framework, where observations make previous information redundant and affect outcomes. It is a world beyond our comprehension because it is a series of glimpses behind which something more appears to be there. Not the hand of God, but the hand of science itself.[231] The more we find out about the physical basis of the world, the more shrouded in mystery that world appears to be. Rovelli in *The Order of Time* points to the mixture of chemical,

---

[230] *Brief Answers to the Big Questions*, page 56

[231] As there is an increasing difficulty in observing and testing below the Planck scale, so there is a greater reliance on mathematical conclusions.

biological and cultural structures which have resulted in us through evolution. Nevertheless, we are "more complex than our mental faculties are capable of grasping. ... We are not even clear about what it means to 'understand.' " [232]

There are at least two different ways of interpreting the initial stages of evolution: firstly, a blind struggle for survival through natural selection alone,[233] secondly, a balance between cellular system self-regulation and natural selection.[234] If a creative intelligence is to be inferred from evolutionary theory, the latter model fits better rather than the former because cellular self-regulation could contain the seeds of more complex forms of social life.[235] To infer the existence of a creative intelligence does not necessarily follow from this, but it hypothetically could assist if cellular self-regulation is interpreted as a forerunner of human society. This, however, would be to make the same mistake that Herbert Spencer made, except in reverse.[236] He thought that evolution laid down the template for understanding human society: to characterise cellular self-regulation as being a divine footprint is equally simplistic. The problem is that we have already seen evolution is not the dominant theory of nature, i.e. it cannot within its own terms explain the theory of relativity or quantum mechanics, so debating whether creativity or blind chance is the basis of life using the theory of evolution is automatically flawed. The uncertainty and incompleteness as to how quantum theory and biology link up is very clearly signalled by Jim Al-Khalili and Jonjoe McFadden when they ask this question: "But is it likely that the strange features of quantum mechanics we have discovered

---

[232] *The Order of Time*, pages 179-80
[233] Dawkin's approach.
[234] Domasio's approach.
[235] This can also be argued in pure evolutionary terms.
[236] See Chapter 3, section entitled 'Evolution and Purpose'.

to be involved in so many crucial phenomena of life are excluded from its most mysterious product, consciousness?"[237]

What does this tell us about our own understanding? A great deal: we are not in a position to present one coherent process which overarches all other theories about life and its origins. In the event of our finding such a theory, the philosophical question would be answered as to whether a creative intelligence behind that process exists. However, scientific intelligence cannot, I believe, rule out the possibility of a creative God because the substance of scientific enquiry at the quantum level is not about cause and effect – it is to do with patterns of action and inaction, appearances and vanishing acts, including predictable and potentially unknowable information. Moreover, it is about the collapse of time, the end of space and the past and future combining. These are not the hallmarks of empirical observation alone – they are the inferences from a combination of mathematical and experimental outcomes which in themselves are changing the concepts we are using to describe the world. They leave in their trail a greater sense of uncertainty than ever before. The concepts they have created, surprisingly, have both a transcendent and an empirical flavour.[238]

We are not conscious of minute changes in time, but they exist and show up mathematically and through specialist observation techniques. Our everyday language uses assumptions about the permanence of space and time inbuilt into the way we see and talk about the world. We can, of course, be forgiven for thinking of time as absolute – relative though it may be, we cannot *elongate time* to prolong our life span even if we can prolong life through advances

---

[237] *Life on the Edge, The Coming of Age of Quantum Biology*, page 352

[238] Richard Dawkins in his book *Outgrowing God* still believes that the laws of physics are of secondary importance to "Darwin and his successors ... solving the bigger problem of life." page 273.

in medical science. Death is a stark reminder of the passage of time. Minute changes in one place compared to another may not be compelling enough to attract our everyday attention, but from a philosophical point of view it is noteworthy that there are many calculations about microscopic states which do not involve time at all.[239]

A world beyond time is a space. A world beyond what we can observe or mathematically predict is a space. A world where information potentially collapses is a space. Nevertheless, many modern writers are not persuaded to use these spaces as inferences for faith because to incorporate faith into the equation simply is using the notion of 'God' as an explanation for the unknown. However, the realisation that our very own scientific achievements, in our perceptions, our observations and mathematical inferences are not objective but a function of the way *we see* the universe, is very significant.[240] If our scientific knowledge is subjective, it does not mean that "God" explains the gaps: it *does* mean that we cannot rely on science *alone* for a complete account of reality.

Mythos and Logos

Should we call science established fact and religion myth? Are they completely separate activities?

In the old world, mythology and ritual had helped people to evoke a sense of sacred significance that had saved them from the void, in rather the same way as did great works of art. But scientific rationalism, the source of Western power and

---

[239] See Rovelli, pg. 151-171.
[240] See Chapter 7, section 'Kant and Reason'.

success, had discredited myth and declared that it alone could lead to truth.[241]

Karen Armstrong does not attempt to minimise the importance of religion – she simply believes there has been a confusion between the empirical methods of science,[242] which she calls 'Logos', with the sense of meaning that religion and spiritual approaches provide: this she refers to as 'Mythos'.[243]

Mythical language could not satisfactorily be translated into rational language without losing its raison d'etre. Like poetry, it contained meanings that were too elusive to be expressed in any other way. *Once theology tried to turn itself into* science, it could only produce a caricature of rational discourse, because these truths are not amenable to scientific demonstration. This spurious religious *logos* would eventually bring religion into further disrepute.[244] (emphasis original)

Karen Armstrong's detailed description in *The Battle for God* analysing developments in Judaism, Islam and Christianity from the 16th century to the beginning of the 21st century graphically shows

---

[241] *The Battle for God*, page 135

[242] This confusion has involved the church becoming embroiled in a competitive struggle with science and liberal theologians who felt the factual tenets of the Christian faith were essentially symbolic: "Religion has to fight for its life against a large class of scientific men, Charles Hodge declared in 1874." *The Battle for God*, page 142.

[243] Karen Armstrong suggests that the resurgence of religious fundamentalism in the late 20th Century is a reaction to the "scientific rationalism of the West." ... it is an attempt to "resacralize an increasingly sceptical world." *The Battle for God*, xi (introduction).

[244] *The Battle for God*, page 141

how the 'science-religion' discourse was, and largely still is, viewed. However, I want to question the contrast Armstrong makes between the 'rational discourse' which typifies science and the 'elusive meanings' which inhabit the world of religion and spirituality. Mythos is meant to be something completely separate from Logos, but then even the most fanciful mythologies have a physiological basis in the brain.[245] For example, understanding the neural mechanisms which accompany a false belief would be seen as scientific work, whilst the belief itself would be perceived as mythology. The difficulty arises in that both 'meaning' and 'social interaction' are necessary requirements in developing an understanding of the relevant neural mechanisms in the first place, regardless of what degree of control those mechanisms may or may not have over the belief itself.

Rovelli, in his book about the journey to quantum gravity, *Reality is Not what it Seems*, writes about the communication between himself and his readers. The atoms in our brains and his own are not disconnected as he is **communicating** with us, his readers.

The world isn't then, just a network of colliding atoms: it is also a network of correlations between sets of atoms, a network of reciprocal information between physical systems. In all of this, there is nothing idealistic or spiritual ... All of this is as much a part of the world as the stones of the Dolomites, the buzzing of bees and the waves of the sea.[246]

---

[245] For a compelling and heartrending account of the interface between the physical and existential domains see *When Breath becomes Air* by Paul Kalanithi. He was a brilliant neurosurgeon who lost his life to cancer at the age of 37 in 2015. He says "to make science the arbiter of metaphysics is to banish not only God from the world but also love, hate, meaning – to consider a world that is self-evidently *not* the world we live in" page 169.

[246] *Reality is Not what it Seems*, pages 213-4

In this quote Rovelli makes the error of saying that a "network of reciprocal information" is the same as saying 'we communicate' The two are bound together but they are not identical. Receiving a signal is not the same as understanding an idea;[247] for Rovelli's account of quantum gravity to have any impact at all on me, I have to read it, digest it and try and understand it. I am doing much more than receiving a signal. I am grasping several concepts. Is this just a semantic difference or is it a central requirement of the development of science? Professor Kip Thorne, in the introduction to *Brief Answers to the Big Questions*, referring to when he took Stephen Hawking and his wife to Moscow, says:

Stephen wowed Zel'dovich and hundreds of other scientists, and in return Stephen learned a thing or two from Zel'dovich … Now, the great value of conversations like this is that they can trigger new directions of thought … one day it triggered a truly radical insight in Stephen's mind: after a black hole stops spinning, the hole can still emit particles.[248]

So, such qualities as imagination and hypothesising are needed for science to progress, but they are not carried out in isolation: they also take place in the context of collaboration and collective knowledge. Once the role of meaning and social interaction is understood to be necessary for science, 'rational empiricism' or Logos must broaden the definition of its own methodology. The results of empirical enquiry are brought about by imagination, collaboration, collective knowledge and theoretical conjecture. However, these also appear to be the ingredients of Mythos. So, what is it that distinguishes Mythos from Logos?

---

[247] See Joelle Proust in first section of Chapter 2.
[248] *Brief Answers to the Big Questions*, xv-xvi

Armstrong's use of the word 'rational' is tied in with the idea of scientific demonstration, i.e. empirical or mathematical proof. Rationality can be associated with empirical success but equally, as we saw in Chapter 4, it can be associated with respect for others. It was suggested there that the word 'rational' is not a neutral word: it often has an implied humanistic connotation involving the wellbeing of others.[249] It is not as easy as she suggests to divorce religion and science through the use of the word 'rational', because the word itself means different things in different contexts. Wittgenstein put it like this: "Language is a labyrinth of paths. You approach it from *one* side and know your way about; you approach the same place from another side and no longer know your way about." [250]

Furthermore, to separate religious meaning from empiricism in the way that Armstrong separates Mythos from Logos is unsustainable because science itself is dependent on both meaning and human interaction for its furtherance. The real differences are the nature of the subject matter and the methodology used to explore issues in question. We may be more successful at progressing science than understanding who we really are because we obtain more concrete results from the former and are prone to greater uncertainty in the latter: those empirical results give us a measurable mastery over nature whilst the latter is harder to quantify and consequently more difficult to isolate in any experimental sense. This does not mean that the significance of human relationships and understanding who we are is of any less importance: qualitative approaches are not inferior to quantitative research methods even if there are more obvious interpretation difficulties in relation to the former.[251]

---

[249] See section 'Rationality as Respect' in Chapter 4.
[250] Philosophical Investigations, page 82e
[251] My thanks to Tim Edwards for raising this point.

The distinction between Mythos and Logos as characterised by Armstrong has connotations of the distinction between a necessary fiction and an incontrovertible non-fiction, but this is a false dichotomy, one she herself acknowledges. There is nothing in scientific enquiry which necessarily implies religion is always false, just as there is nothing in religion preventing open-minded scientific enquiry. Science and religion are different avenues of enquiry into the significance of the world and our place in it. Just as the quest for the truth about the natural world through science can be flawed, so the search for meaning and significance in our personal lives can also be flawed. The achievements of one do not rule out the value of the other. Just because human beings are sometimes very cruel through the exercise of their religion and sometimes obviously wrong about certain religious claims, it does not mean that religion itself is always a mistaken pursuit. In the same way, scientific activity is not wrong just because science is used to inflict destruction on people and the natural world and false or incomplete theories are pursued. Making mistakes in the application of a scientific skill, social practice or religious approach is not a sufficient reason to stop the practices altogether: it is a reason to do things differently, and for that a moral and social context is required.

A Space for Faith

What does science actually do for us?

How can science be contrasted with religion? Not through the significance of meaning, social collaboration, imagination and speculative hypothesising: these are common to both. The methodologies are, however, very different: should I be troubled about my sense of purpose in life I am unlikely to start doing mathematical equations – I might, if I am so inclined, go to other people for help, professional or personal, or even pray. On the other hand, if I am a physicist working on quantum gravity, I am unlikely to ask a priest how I should conduct my investigations: I am more than likely to use the scientific methods at my disposal.

Science, unless I am directly involved in it as part of my own life, does not provide me with any sense of relationship – it is not a person, it is not a family, it is not a community: religion provides that kind of fulfilment for many. For those who do not practise religion, science still does not fulfil their need for satisfying personal relationships. What science does, whether I am directly involved in it or not, is provide me with greater technical mastery over my environment through the consumer products and medical advances derived from it.

It is in seeing the limitations of science rather than viewing it as a replacement for religion that a more realistic perspective is achieved.[252] Once the impersonal basis of science is acknowledged, spaces for the more personal and spiritual aspects of living present themselves more readily.

---

[252] I am indebted to Tim Edwards for raising the substance of the following point. In modern living we are encouraged to reduce lifestyle features (e.g. diet) to a series of measurable outcomes. Something like diet might be affected by, or indicate, so much more than simply what food we eat and how much – it'll also entail our human relationships, how we think and feel about ourselves, our economic and social circumstances, the availability of resources etc. To suggest that we can address this more holistic life by measuring the number of steps we take each day is, notwithstanding the latter's usefulness, perhaps to begin to reduce life to the status of an overly simplistic 'empirical' science. Such is the increasing pressure to address qualitative values (e.g. 'a sense of purpose in life') as if they were simply quantifiable (e.g. enumerating 'goals' and listing ways of achieving them, and by when...).

A Poem by Tim Edwards

This vortice, doubt
might burgeon into faith.

Can I lie? – even one
without horizon
must, of what's given,
form not a garden
but a universe
constant in the making –

grit, worked until
a rim of light appears
beyond possible doubt,
impossible faith:

the trust necessary
to a proper understanding

Chapter 11
Conclusion (2) – Human Nature – Can We Go It Alone?

I have argued that if mistakes in the practice of science and religion are made, as they invariably are, those mistakes do not necessarily mean that science and religion should be abandoned. They provide an incentive to carry out the activities differently: it follows that *changes* are required to those activities, at least from the viewpoint of the person who believes a mistake has been made. So, on occasions when scientific knowledge is used to inflict torture on victims, it *is* a misuse of that knowledge. It follows that *limits* then have to be placed on how such knowledge is used. We also, by implication, promote *standards* to aspire to when it comes to the application of that knowledge. Alternatively, when religious belief is used as a vehicle to oppress or put people at a disadvantage, both *limits* preventing such behaviour and *standards* to aspire to are implied. The paradox is that in many cases these were the original aspirations of the religion itself. That means we need a *wider context* for the practice of both science and religion to take place in because we know they are sometimes instrumental in practices which we instantly recoil against, judging them to be inhumane. Our sense of what is 'inhumane' is, in turn, related to our own moral sensibilities.[253]

---

[253] Appendix 2 explains how I am using the term 'moral'.

Coming to Terms with Human Nature as Evolution Has Formed it – Is There a Single View?

Stephen Pinker underlines the natural tendency human beings have towards strife through retracing our genetic origins, explaining that conflict, altruism and evolution all go together: they are inextricably part of one another. He believes we should turn the negative aspects of our genetic inheritance into positive characteristics. In his book, *The Blank State*, he says:

> But we fight those afflictions not by denying the pesky facts of nature but by turning some of them against others ... And for the efforts to be humane, they must acknowledge the universal pleasures and pains that make some kinds of change desirable.[254]

Being loyal and caring to our own kin is, in effect, an unconscious method of preserving our own gene pool. It is underlaid by a biological drive which centres on self-preservation. Joshua Greene says that this mechanism is part and parcel of the natural world. The difference is that some organisms are more conscious of it than others:

> Among humans, of course, caring behaviour is motivated by feelings, including powerful emotional bonds that connect us to our close relatives. Thus, familial love is more than just a warm and fuzzy thing. It's a strategic biological device, a piece

---

[254] *The Blank Slate. The Modern Denial of Human Nature*, pages 172-3

of moral machinery that enables genetically related individuals to reap the benefits of cooperation.[255]

With this view of human nature we are at war with ourselves, using the 'survival at all costs' instinct to see the benefit of more altruistic ways of social interaction. However, as already mentioned in Chapter 6, there is another variant at play in early evolutionary theory, namely cooperation.

Peter Godfrey-Smith, a marine biologist and philosopher, describes the early seeds of social behaviour.

Bacteria are one among several kinds of single cell life, and they are simpler in many ways than the cells that eventually came together to make animals ... Biologists who work on these organisms are more and more inclined to see the senses of bacteria as attuned to the presence and activities of other cells around them ... This may not sound like much, but it opens an important door. Once the same chemicals are being sensed and produced, there is the possibility of coordination between cells. We have reached the birth of social behaviour.[256]

Here we have a second alternative view of human nature with cooperation embedded in it from the earliest beginnings – it is not the story of a blind struggle for survival we are so accustomed to. This observation is irrespective of any inference about a creative intelligence behind it. Greene, however, says "the natural world is full of cooperation, from tiny cells to packs of wolves. But all of this teamwork, however impressive, evolved for the amoral purpose

---

[255] *Moral Tribes – Emotion, Reason, and the Gap Between Us and Them*, page 31
[256] *Other Minds, The Octopus and the Evolution of Intelligent Life*, page 18

of successful competition." [257] Greene doesn't know this: it is an assumption. There are many ways of assessing what human nature is and the dogma that has followed on from 'The Blind Watchmaker' model is no longer the only model to consider.[258]

Take, for example, the idea of merging the idea of quantum theory with broader notions. This position is summed up eloquently by Tim Edwards, my friend who has helped me throughout this book, in this hitherto unpublished remark. He takes the notion of what Greene calls a "global tribe that looks out for its members ... simply because it's good" [259] and connects it with more recent scientific developments:

Hence, these two broad areas of scientific focus – artificial selection and quantum subjectivity – appear to hold out the promise of a way of being for humanity that's not defined solely by scientific humanism or by an assumed metaphysical warrant for hope/faith, but by something that partakes of and yet transcends both. One way, possibly, of characterising the *modus* of this way of being is that of 'rational intuition' – a way of being whose immanence in human creativity will establish a template for future development in which the integrity of the ethical with the epistemological will comprehend what's currently compartmentalised: the scientific, the spiritual, the moral/ethical and the social/political.

When natural selection first became known, human nature was described as brutal, blind and unthinking; now we know more about self-regulation systems and sensing qualities in cells, we are

---

[257] *Moral Tribes – Emotion, Reason, and the Gap Between Us and Them*, page 363
[258] See Chapter 5 – Something from Nothing.
[259] *Moral Tribes – Emotion, Reason, and the Gap Between Us and Them*, page 363

incorporating cooperation into the description of human nature. Further models are now emerging which, like Tim Edwards' example, centre around human creativity. Although natural selection is a powerful narrative about the origin of our species, it is no longer a full enough explanation to justify our experience of it and, furthermore, it is no longer the overriding dominant influence. What is being advanced is that we have begun to outrun the biological forces inherent in natural selection.

Knowledge and its Rate of Growth

Human agency is changing our genetic history as well as destabilising the external environment through our own burgeoning consumption patterns. We could survive on much less than we do in our modern democratic society, and if we did our planet would be in a healthier state, but our genes have not yet received this signal. Will they receive it in due time? Stephen Hawking's prediction is the theme that the human race will probably not be able to stop itself, as a species, from ravaging the planet despite the actions of some far-sighted individuals. Even more dramatically, Stephen Hawking predicts in *Brief Answers to the Big Questions* that in all likelihood we will have to leave this planet: "We are running out of space and the only places to go to are other worlds." [260]

There is no 'self-control gene' that stops us wanting more and more materially. The only solution for governments to be successfully elected appears to be for parties to promise increasing economic growth: political success could be environmental disaster. At the time of writing, there is a great deal of political concern about how much time is left to change consumer habits and manufacturing processes.

---

[260] *Brief Answers to the Big Questions*, page 149

Furthermore, knowledge itself is a form of political power. Stephen Hawking says:

> Laws will probably be passed against genetic engineering with humans. But some people won't be able to resist the temptation to improve human characteristics, such as memory, resistance to disease and length of life. Once such superhumans appear, there are going to be major political problems with the unimproved humans who won't be able to compete.[261]

Harari puts the situation in more graphic terms, adding his own theory that we are creating systems that could eventually outsmart the human race:

> If scientific discoveries and technological developments split humankind into a mass of useless humans and a small elite of upgraded superhumans, or if authority shifts altogether away from human beings into the hands of highly intelligent algorithms,[262] then liberalism will collapse.[263]

If the theory of natural selection is only a partial explanation of the survival of our species where intelligence has now *outrun* our capacity for self-control, the theory itself is of little use in going forward: a theory which explains the past but not the future will not help us determine the best outcomes for the human race. Under natural selection, species survival was brought about by fortuitous

---

[261] Ibid, page 81

[262] Tim Edwards points out that this argument is a variant of the 'cold alien' motif in the science fiction of the earlier 20th century.

[263] *Sapiens*, page 408

changes which provided the means to master new surroundings. Under artificial selection, genetic changes which can bring about population restraint, restoring the ecosystem, moderation in consumption and in the use of fossil fuels are currently running very late if they are to protect our species from itself. In the terms of the original theory, such changes would need to morph back into our own genetic structure.

International cooperation on climate change appears to be a fragile edifice: national interests, the desire for economic growth, competitive trading, disagreements about the science of global warming and the relative influence of human activity against planetary changes are all critical factors, many of which are disputed as to their significance for the wellbeing of the species. It is beyond this piece of work to provide a detailed analysis of whether the glass is half full or half empty. Nevertheless, in a world of over 7 billion people, it is impossible to arrive at a definitive answer as to whether species survival is more important to people than national, community or family interests. We can no longer rely on natural selection to do the job for us: the collective actions we take will substantially affect the longevity of our own species.

Transcendence – Is it relevant?

The notion that belief in a transcendent deity is of any substantive relevance as far as the destiny of the human race is concerned is dismissed by modern writers. Nevertheless, I would contend that even the most radical atheist would soften should they become convinced that there **actually** was a higher level of moral existence than that which we can fathom for ourselves. This would **not** imply a suspension of human moral activity, but an increased awareness that our own judgements can be limited and sometimes fallible. The sense I am deriving from the term 'higher moral being' is indeed based on my own Christian faith but it is, for me, one of deriving inspiration, accepting my own limitations but at the same time using all my energy and knowledge to achieve positive outcomes for other people. It is not one of a subservient, 'serf-like' dependence on other people's interpretations which I may or may not understand, perhaps delivered by people who exercise social, political and religious power over me, neither is it solely one of a remote court of appeal for complex and difficult cases. It is, to put it colloquially, about doing our best while, at the same time, accepting our limitations. We can do this without a belief in a deity who has identified with humankind, but it is also possible to do it with such a belief.[264]

However, even before considering the possibility of a higher moral authority there has to be a basis for believing that transcendence is part of reality. As Jon Cartwright's 2019 article 'Something from Nothing' from the *New Scientist* says, "There is a chance virtual particles could start transforming into real ones at lower laser intensities." [265]

The point is that at the same time as dismissing transcendence as an outdated anachronism of a past mythological age, researchers into quantum electrodynamics are talking about the concept of virtual particles "transforming" into real ones.[266] The assumption that reality is confined to a concrete physicality is now being challenged by science itself. The belief that the world is essentially and only physically concrete has become a culturally accepted norm in the developed world and this is mainly due to the success of scientific

---

[264] There are two separate issues here: firstly, whether there is a need for a deeper sense of moral awareness in human affairs and secondly, whether there is a case to argue that there is any convincing moral teaching from a divine source. It is of course possible to accept the first without the second. The problem then is where to find that deeper sense of moral awareness.

[265] *New Scientist*, Vol. 241, No. 3214, Jan 2019, pages 42-3

[266] Ibid, pages 42-3

enterprise in the modern era. I would suggest we have rushed to draw universal conclusions about the nature of the world prematurely, particularly from the idea of natural selection. Every time we reach a point where we think we have reached the edge of what there is to know, we are confounded by new discoveries. Now we have a form of transcendence within science itself. However, there are still deep reservations about the ill effects of religion.

How can religious convictions about God be compatible with religious tolerance?

Science is not a neutral activity: knowledge is applied, and for that a moral context is required. Religion has purported to provide that context with very mixed results. The problem in mixing faith with morality is that it has often resulted in unacceptable forms of social control, sometimes involving abuse, all justified in the name of God. The history of the church and state working in tandem is littered with accounts of intolerance, repression and the reinforcing of existing power structures.[267]

The risk attached to 'Mythos', to use Karen Armstrong's terminology, is the potential for abuse when religious beliefs are used as a means of social control. So how can this issue be addressed? I want to refer back to the 'rationality for respect' concept promoted by Immanuel Kant. Robert Wicks, quoting Kant, says this: "Act only according to that maxim whereby you can at the same time will that it should become a universal law." [268] Wicks continues, again including a further quote: "Yet another way to express the categorical imperative is to require that we always respect the humanity in ourselves and in everyone else. This yields a third formulation of the categorical imperative,

---

[267] As already mentioned, Appendix 3 outlines some examples.
[268] *Kant, A Complete Introduction*, page 154

expressive of the dignity of the human being: 'act so that you treat humanity, whether in your own person or in that of another, in every case as an end and never as a means only.' " [269]

Kant's application of rationality is about respect for persons. Consider the idea that you always behave in a way that you would want everyone to. If, for example, you adopt the rule never to lie because you don't want to be lied to, then lying to protect someone's feelings is problematic – two brothers decide to tell their little sister that her father died of a heart attack when in fact he committed suicide because he had lost all his money through ill-advised business transactions.[270] Were they acting against a universal law of respect for others? Obviously not, but they were contravening the rule about never lying. So, the rule then becomes 'never lie unless you consider it in the subject's best interest to manipulate the truth for the sake of their welfare'. This means that it is a contravention of the rule to tell a lie for the benefit of your *own* feelings. The problem arises as to whether the two brothers were telling their sister that the father had had a heart attack for their sister's benefit *or* their own feelings *or* both – if both, the purpose would be to protect the sister's feelings *and* make life more tolerable for the brothers themselves. The problem arises as to which was the greater of the two influences: the difficulty is in formulating a rule which can distinguish the relative strengths of the two motivations.[271] Exploring various avenues of motivation is not a precise science and it often takes time to even formulate possible alternatives.

---

[269] Ibid, page 156

[270] This example is taken from a real family history.

[271] It could be argued that psychological testing could measure the relative strengths of the two contrasting motives. However, it is not practically possible to 'freeze' social interactions to assess motivation in the normal course of everyday life.

So, the problem with the categorical imperative is not just deciding what the content of universal rules should be but isolating the various motivations and influences which centre on any action which is taken. Formulating an absolute rule is relatively easy compared to trying to apply it in the mix of genetic, environmental, historical and cultural influences which bear down upon our actual lives. However, once conditional clauses are applied to universal rules, the rules themselves become increasingly complex and when this happens, they become very hard to internally process and apply without error. Some corners of our legal system involving case law precedent are clear examples of his kind of difficulty.

So how does this apply to religion? Take, for example, the Christian idea that genuine faith should be based on free choice. What is the universal rule of respect for others which applies in this circumstance? In Christian terms this is embodied in "Love your neighbour as yourself." In Kantian terms, it is to treat everyone else as an end not a means. The key question relating to the idea of individual choice in relation to faith is this: what degree of persuasive argument is legitimate before the 'choice' an individual makes is, in fact, a part or full capitulation to social pressure? Secondly, how much freedom of choice is there to leave a community of faith? This, surely, is also a problem that applies in politics and for other institutions in society.

I would suggest that the more *genuine* a choice is made available to the individual *inside* the faith community, the more religious tolerance is adhered to on an *external* basis. The problem in faith groups is that they often cannot reconcile religious toleration with a strong belief that they are in possession of the truth.[272] The difficulty

---

[272] This appears to apply to sections of all religious groups even where there are scriptures which say people should be allowed to practice their own faith, e.g. "There is no compulsion where the religion is concerned" (Holy Quran: 2/256).

for many may be that they identify themselves to be like divine civil servants rather than divine subjects. A civil servant should only think to the limit of what his or her political master wants. However, in being a divine subject is far easier for me to hold firm convictions but also maintain an awareness that I may be wrong in terms of *my* own perceptions – as a divine emissary this option is less available. To say, 'I believe x is the truth but I don't fully understand it' is very different from saying 'I believe x is the truth and I understand *all* the implications of that truth'. It is not the subject matter which determines whether we 'know' all there is to know about it: rather, it is where we place ourselves on the 'ladder' of knowledge that counts. Are we 'masters' *over* or 'participant observers' *within* that knowledge? If we have a foot on the bottom rung of a ladder, do we know what the view is from the top? Are there other places which we have not yet reached? This positioning applies to both science and religion even though their methodologies are very different from one another.

So why do we need to refer to a higher moral authority than our own if religion has so many pitfalls? In short, our natures are fallible. Furthermore, we are more than rational beings – complex in terms of all the influences that exert themselves on us and also in terms of the influences which we ourselves exert on others and the natural world. The space for faith has to be tied in with a higher moral authority than our own, otherwise our aspirations are more likely to become individually centred, whereas they should be balanced between our own needs, those of others, and the natural world itself.

We saw in the first section that within quantum gravity research lies the principle that our own scientific observations and calculations are inevitably integrated into the knowledge we are seeking. The same can be said of other areas of life, including our relationships and religious beliefs. This is not to say that everything is internal to ourselves, but it is to acknowledge that we cannot assume we fully know the mind of a deity or even another person beyond us. The Christian account is that God has revealed Himself in the person of Christ. This does not mean that followers of Christ know the mind of God. Consequently, we should be tolerant: our firm beliefs are firm, but they are also subject to our own limitations. It is the same principle that applies to human relationships: we connect with each other, sometimes very closely, but we can never fully enter into the mind of another person.

A Concluding Thought

As the assumptions behind science are explored, so the spaces for faith seem to reveal themselves. The deepest areas of quantum physics have to incorporate subjectivity as playing a fundamental role in the research project. Whilst embracing reason, we have also to acknowledge the inadequacy of reason alone to solve the moral problems of our age. Concepts and social collaboration play a critical role in the manipulation of genetics and, finally, the disjunction between the growth of knowledge and the wisdom of how to use it without plunging the planet into an early grave are pointers towards a direction that hitherto we have been persuaded to ignore. There is no formulaic solution, but even though we see in a glass darkly we should still face the glass rather than turn away from it.

The place of the 'person' is as significant as the role of the electron and may turn out to be more so. I cannot place my faith in a far-removed deity any more than I can in the bounce of a black hole into a white hole.[273] For faith to have any purchase on my life, that distant

---

[273] See Penrose, R (2010) Cycles of Time (GB: Bodley Head) pg. 125 for Rovelli, C (15.12.2018) 'In Search of White Holes', *New Scientist* Vol 240, No. 3208, pg. 30-3.

deity has to show me what it is to be human. This is where the life of Christ, for me, comes in – for the atheist or agnostic reader that may be something to ponder but I hope that the arguments in this book will help anyone, including me, from assuming they know more than they do.

Postscript

My overall objective in this book was to try and put myself in the shoes of an agnostic even though I am a practising Christian. I wanted to see where the arguments would lead me. There is probably no such thing as absolute neutrality but there is no shame in trying. As we discover more about the way the natural world and our own species works, it may seem perplexing to include an invisible deity which might form part of a coherent worldview, especially if your instincts don't send you in that direction.

Within the human context there are a range of positions concerning transcendence which are taken, and I have included some short comments from my friend Tim Edwards in the final chapter which represent a different kind of transcendence in a purely human context. Despite this being a different stance from the one I have chosen to represent, I respect Tim's approach to life and wanted to give him a voice, especially given the enormous help he has been in developing this piece of work. There is, however, an even more important reason which is that unless we are prepared to listen to other people, we may never discover the weaknesses in our own position.

As things stand, there is no intellectual case to either prove or disprove the existence of God. It is, however, possible to conceive of intelligent design through our own increasing ability to intervene in and change natural processes. However, this is not just an argument about intelligent design – it is about inner change. Many do not wish for a further frame of reference than ourselves and our own potential; others, like me, find such a position both intellectually and spiritually wanting.

For me the life, teaching, suffering and overcoming of death by someone who claimed to be both human and divine is worth the risk of faith – the experience of having faith in the person and character of a God through the teachings and life of Christ has been a gift. It has not made me immune from the trials of life, but it has given me strength and a sense that it does not all end with me. In practising such faith, I assume no superiority whatsoever over anyone else nor any predictive capacity about the future in this life or thereafter. I also know that I cannot *empirically* demonstrate the legitimacy of faith. Different kinds of knowledge are equally valid but are tested and experienced in very different ways.

References

Alexander, D, *Creation or Evolution, Do We Have To Choose?* Monarch Publishing, Oxford, 2008.

Anderson, JND, *The Evidence for the Resurrection.* InterVarsity Press, Nottingham, England, 1966. Also there is an online version at *https://biblicalstudies.org.uk/article_resurrection_anderson.html* (Accessed 25 May 2018)

Al-Khalili, J & McFadden, J, *Life on the Edge, The Coming of Age of Quantum Biology.* Penguin, Random House, United Kingdom 2014.

Anne Frank – In The Secret Annexe – who was who? Anne Frank House, Amsterdam, 2013

Armstrong, K *The Battle for God.* Harper Perennial, London, 2000.

Armstrong K, *Islam, A Short History.* Phoenix Press, London 2009.

Aurelius, M, *Meditations.* Translated by Martin Hammond, Penguin Random House, London, 2014.

Ball, P, "Reality? It's what you make it." *New Scientist*, Vol. 236, No. 3151, Nov 2017.

Bennett, J. *Rationality, An Essay towards Analysis*. Routledge and Keegan Paul, London, 1964.

Blackford, R and Schuklenk, U, *50 Great Myths about Atheism*. Wiley Blackwell, Chichester, 2013.

Broadie, A, *The Scottish Enlightenment*, Birlinn, Edinburgh, 2007.

Broome, J, *Rationality Through Reasoning*, Wiley Blackwell, Oxford, 2013.

Bruce, FF, *The New Testament Documents, Are They Reliable?* Bottom of the Hill Publishing, 2013.

Bryant, L, *Difference and Givenness; Deleuze's Transcendental Empiricism and the Ontology of Immanence*. Northwestern University Press, Illinois, 2008.

Byrie, A, *Protestants, The Radicals who made the Modern World*. William Collins, London, 2017.

Cain, S, *Quiet, The Power of Introverts in a World That Can't Stop Talking*. Penguin, New York, 2012.

Cartwright, J, "Something from Nothing." *New Scientist*, Vol. 241, No. 3214, Jan 2019.

Case Study: Apartheid, ReQuest, *http://request.org.uk/issues/social-issues/case-study-apartheid/* (Accessed 22 March 2018)

Churchland, P, "Why do we care?" *New Scientist,* Vol. 243, No. 3249, Sept 2019.

Clutton-Brock, T, "Cooperation between non-kin in animal societies." *Nature,* Vol. 462, Macmillan, Nov 2009.

Cohn, N, *The Pursuit of the Millennium.* Secker & Warburg, London, 1957.

Cockcroft, D, reproduced with kind permission from Seeds of the Kingdom, 23 July 2016, in CSM (Creation Science Movement) Journal, "Migrating Insects." *Creation: Journal of the CSM Movement,* Vol. 19, Feb 2017, *https://www.genesisexpo.org.uk/csm-journal-vol-19-no-5-february-2017/* (Accessed on 2 March 2018)

Connor, S, "World exclusive: human embryos genetically altered for first time with new technology." *iNews,* 2017, *https://inews.co.uk/news/health/world-exclusive-human-embryos-genetically-altered-first-time-new-technology/* (Accessed 21 March 19)

Darwin Correspondence Project, "Letter no.12041." *https://www.darwinproject.ac.uk/letter/DCP-LETT-12041.xml* (Accessed 11 September 2019)

Darwin, C, *The Autobiography of Charles Darwin. 1809-1882.* Norton and Company, London 1969

Dawkins, R, *The God Delusion.* Bantam Press, London, 2006.

Dawkins, R, *The Greatest Show on Earth, The Evidence for Evolution.* Free Press, New York, 2009.

Dawkins, R, *Outgrowing God – A Beginner's Guide*. Penguin Random House, London, 2019.

De Bellaigue, C, *The Islamic Enlightenment, The Modern Struggle between Faith and Reason*. Penguin, London, 2017.

Dennett, D, *From Bacteria to Bach and Back – the Evolution of Minds*. Penguin Random House, London, 2017.

Domasio, A, *Looking for Spinoza, Joy, Sorrow and the Feeling Brain*. Vintage Books, London, 2004.

Domasio, A, *The Strange Order of Things*. Pantheon, New York, 2018.

Du Sautoy, M, *What We Cannot Know*. Harper Collins, London, 2016.

Gettier, E, "Is Justified, True Belief Knowledge?" *Analysis*, Vol. 23, 1963. Found at *fitelson.org/proseminar/**gettier**.pdf* (Accessed 26 January 2018)

Gilbertson, J, "Frozen boy: 10 years after being brought back to life." *CBS Minnesota*, 2011, *http://minnesota.cbslocal.com/2011/02/03/ frozen-boy-10-years-after-being-brought-back-to-life/* (Accessed 28 May 2018)

Godfrey-Smith, P, *Other Minds, The Octopus and the Evolution of Intelligent Life*. William Collins, London, 2017.

Gottlieb, A, *The Dream of Enlightenment, The Rise of Modern Philosophy*. Penguin Random House, London, 2016.

Grayling, AC, *What is Good? The Search for the Best Way to Live.* Phoenix, London, 2003.

Greene, J, *Moral Tribes – Emotion, Reason, and the Gap Between Us and Them.* Atlantic, London, 2013.

Gregg, HS, *The Causes of Religious Wars: Holy Nations, Sacred Spaces, and Religious Revolutions* (Unpublished doctoral dissertation). Massachusetts Institute of Technology, 2004. Found at *https://dspace.mit.edu/bitstream/handle/1721.1/16639/56191324-MIT.pdf?sequence=2* (Accessed 26 March 2018)

Harari, YN, *Sapiens.* Penguin Random House, London, 2011.

Haught, J.F, *God and the New Atheism: a critical response to Dawkins, Harris and Hitchens.* Louisville KY: Westminster John Knox Press, 2008.

Hawking, S, "The Origin of the Universe." 2005, *http://www.hawking.org.uk/the-origin-of-the-universe.html* (Accessed 21.3.2019)

Hawking, S, *A Brief History of Time.* Penguin Random House, London, 2016.

Hawking, S, *Brief Answers to the Big Questions.* Spacetime Publications, London, 2018.

Hitchens, C, *god is not Great, How Religion Poisons Everything.* Twelve, New York, 2007.

Hume, D, A *Treatise of Human Nature*. Penguin Classics, London, 1985 (first published 1739).

Horowitz, MC "Long time going: Religion and the duration of crusading." *International Security*, Vol. 34, No. 2, 2009.

Jarvie, IC *Rationality and Relativism, In search of a philosophy and history of anthropology*. Routledge, Oxford, 1984.

Jones, S, *Evolution (A Ladybird Expert Book)*. Penguin Random House, London, 2017.

Jones, S, *In the Blood – God, Genes and Destiny*. Flamingo, United Kingdom, 1996.

Kalanithi, P, *When Breath Becomes Air*. Penguin Random House, London, 2016.

Kang, DC "Why was there no religious war in premodern East Asia?" *European Journal of International Relations*, Vol. 20, No. 4, 2014.

Kant, I, *The Answer to the Question: What is Enlightenment?* Translated by H.B. Nisbet, Penguin, London, 1991.

Kemp-Smith, N, *A Commentary to Kant's 'Critique of Pure Reason'*. Macmillan, London, 1918.

Knapton, S, "Huntington's breakthrough as early trial shows injection may stop disease." *Daily Telegraph*, December 2017, *http://www. telegraph.co.uk/science/2017/12/11/huntingtons-breakthrough-early-trials-show-injection-may-stop/* (Accessed 13 December 2017)

Levin, R, "A Defence of Objectivity." *The Theory of Knowledge, Classical and Contemporary Readings*, Second Edition, Wadsworth, International Thomson Publishing, USA, 1999.

Macintyre, A, *Whose Justice? Which Rationality?* Duckworth, London, 1988.

Muluk, H, Sumaktoyo, NG, & Ruth, DM, "Jihad as justification: National survey evidence of belief in violent jihad as a mediating factor for sacred violence among Muslims in Indonesia." *Asian Journal of Social Psychology*, Vol. 16, No. 2, 2013.

O'Brien, D, *An Introduction to the Theory of Knowledge.* 2nd Edition, Polity Press, Cambridge, 2017.

Ostenfield, E, *Ancient Greek Psychology and the Modern Mind-Body Debate*, Aarhus University Press, Denmark, 1987.

Pant, A, "Wood frog dies and comes back to life." *Awesci*, http://awesci. com/wood-frog-dies-and-comes-back/ (Accessed 28 May 2018)

Paisner, M, "Gettier and Justified True Belief." *University of Maryland*, 2012, *https://www.cs.umd.edu/class/fall2012/cmsc828d/ oldreportfiles/paisner2.pdf* (Accessed 16 January 2018)

Penrose, R, "Roger Penrose's Cycle of Universes." *Radio National*, October 2016, *http://www.abc.net.au/radionational/programs/scienceshow/roger-penrose's-cycle-of-universes/7955860#transcript* (Accessed 6 October 2018)

Pinker, S, *The Blank Slate. The Modern Denial of Human Nature*, Penguin, London, 2002.

Pinker, S, *Enlightenment Now. The Case for Reason, Science and Humanism*, Penguin Random House, London, 2018.

Proust, J, "The Evolution of Primate Communication and Metacommunication." *Mind and Language*, Vol. 31, No. 2, WILEY Blackwell, 2016.

"Replicating Milgram's Obedience Experiment – yet again." The Situationist, 2009. *https://thesituationist.wordpress.com/2009/09/10/ replicating-milgrams-obedience-experiment-yet-again/*. See also *http://news.bbc.co.uk/1/hi/health/7791278.stm* (Accessed 14 March 2018)

Rölli, M, "Immanence and Transcendence." *Bulletin de la Societé Américaine de Philosophie de Langue Français*, Vol. 14, No. 2, Fall 2004.

Romey, K, "The Real Jesus." *National Geographic*, Vol. 232, No. 6, 2017.

Rovelli, C, *Seven Brief Lessons on Physics*. Penguin Random House, London, 2014.

Rovelli, C, *The Order of Time*. Penguin Random House, London, 2018.

Rovelli, C, "In Search of White Holes." *New Scientist*, Vol. 240, No. 3208, Dec 2018.

Russell, B (1927) "Why I am not a Christian." A full transcript can be obtained at *https://users.drew.edu/jlenz/whynot.html* (Accessed 9 February 2018)

Russell, B, *History of Western Philosophy*. Routledge, London and New York, 1946.

Sellars, W, *Empiricism and the Philosophy of Mind*. Harvard University Press, Massachusetts, 1997.

Sherlock, M, "The Atheist Atrocities Fallacy — Hitler, Stalin, and Pol Pot." *Areo Magazine*, 2017, *https://areomagazine.com/2017/02/17/the-atheist-atrocities-fallacy-hitler-stalin-and-pol-pot/25* (Accessed 23 March 2019)

Singer, P, *The Expanding Circle: Ethics and Socio-Biology*, Oxford University Press, 1981.

Spencer, H, *The Principles of Sociology Vol 1-2*. D Appleton and Company, New York, 1897.

Stanovitch, K, *Who is Rational? Studies of Individual Differences in Reasoning*. Routledge, Hove, 1999.

Sterenly, K, *Thought in a Hostile World; The Evolution of Human Cognition*. Blackwell, Oxford, 2003.

Svensson, I, "Conflict and Peace." *Handbook of Religion and Society*, Handbooks of Sociology and Social Research, Springer International Publishing, Switzerland, 2016.

Tallis, R & Eagleman, D "The Brain… it makes you think. Doesn't it?" *The Guardian*, 2012, *https://www.theguardian.com/science/2012/*

apr/29/neuroscience-david-eagleman-raymond-tallis (Accessed 10 April 2017)

"Thalidomide." *Brought to Life: Exploring the History of Medicine,* Science Museum, *http://broughttolife.sciencemuseum.org.uk/ broughttolife/themes/controversies/thalidomide* (Accessed 13 October 2017)

Van Whyhe, J, "Was Charles Darwin an Atheist?" *The Public Domain Review,* 2011, *https://publicdomainreview.org/2011/06/28/was-charles-darwin-an-atheist/* (Accessed 28 May 2017)

Vallejo-Marin, M, "Isles 'monkey flower' is a new species." *Shetland Times,* 2017, *https://www.shetlandtimes.co.uk/2017/08/16/isles-monkey-flower-new-species* (Accessed 22 March 2019)

Verhoef, A, "Embodied religion's radicalisation of immanence and the consequent question of transcendence." *Acta Academia,* Vol. 45, No. 4, 2013.

Weiss, I, "The Largest Prime Number Ever Discovered Stretches to Millions of Digits. But Why do We Need to Know About It?" *The I Newspaper,* 2018.

Whiston, W and Maier, P, *The Revised and Expanded Edition of the New Complete Works of Josephus.* Kregel, United States, 1999.

Wicks, R, *Kant, A Complete Introduction.* Hodder and Stoughton, London, 2014.

Williams, B, *Ethics and the Limits of Philosophy.* Collins/Fontana, London, 1985.

Winch, P, *The Idea of a Social Science and its Relation to Philosophy*. Routledge & Kegan Paul, London, 1958.

Wittgenstein, L, *Philosophical Investigations*. 3rd edition, Basil Blackwell, Oxford, 1967.

Appendix 1

The Resurrection – a Flight of Fancy?

| Is the idea of resurrection a myth without any scientific credibility? |

It is fairly clear from the following passage in 1 Corinthians 15 that the gospel or good news about Christ for the apostles was dependent on an actual belief in the resurrection, and that as early as around AD 56 people were expressing scepticism about such a possibility. St Paul said this in his letter to the Corinthian church:

> But if it is preached, that Christ has been raised from the dead, how can some of you say that there is no resurrection of the dead? If there is no resurrection of the dead, then not even Christ has been raised. And if Christ has not been raised, our preaching is useless and so is your faith. More than that, we are then found to be false witnesses about God, for we have testified about God that He raised Christ from the dead. But he did not raise him if in fact the dead are not raised. For if the dead are not raised, then Christ has not been raised either. And if Christ has not been raised, your faith is futile; you are still in your sins. Then those also who have fallen asleep in Christ are lost. If only for this life we have hope in Christ, we are to be pitied more than all men. (1 Corinthians 15:12-20)

It is noteworthy that even in that pre-scientific age, the idea of resurrection was an anathema to everything most people felt about the way the world worked. Those who did believe were "to be pitied more than all men." (1 Corinthians 15:19)if it could be shown to be false. In our age, it is hard-edged materialism combined with an evidence-based approach to rational enquiry which tends to rule out any possibility of such manifestations as bodily resurrection. The idea of resurrection has obvious connotations of being anti-scientific, and therefore counts as 'myth'.

It was, however, not the resurrection on its own that impelled the confused disciples to suddenly turn around and leave Jerusalem for distant parts to preach the Christian Gospel. Firstly, immediately after the resurrection, they did not know what they should do. It was over a period of time that they encountered the risen Christ and then at Pentecost, sometime after they had seen Christ for the last time, they became totally single-minded about spreading the Gospel and building local communities of Christians.

A second reason why resurrection itself was not considered sufficient to qualify someone for divine status was the raising of Lazarus, a close friend of Christ, as recorded in John's Gospel.[274] There are no references to Lazarus being venerated. The resurrection of Christ is inextricably linked to His claim that he was God incarnate and that God expressed his love for people through the pain and sacrifice of the cross. "For even the Son of Man did not come to be served, but to serve, and to give his life as a ransom for many" (St. Mark's Gospel 10:45). The resurrection was about more than

---

[274] The main thrust of this section depends on the authenticity of the New Testament Documents. I rely on FF Bruce's book *The New Testament Documents – Are They Reliable?*

someone coming back to life: after several meetings with various disciples, Christ is said to have ascended into heaven.

There are two main objections to the resurrection of Christ as historical fact: one is psychological and circumstantial, and the other is scientific. In terms of the former, a powerful defence against this sceptical view is the short book *The Evidence For The Resurrection* by JND Anderson, who was like FF Bruce a committed Christian; he used his legal training to assess the historical circumstances around the claim that Christ had risen from the dead.[275] In relation to the scientific questions, at the end of his account, Anderson says this:

Some critic may object that a resurrection from the dead is so incredible that no amount of evidence would suffice. (Such an attitude seems prejudiced and unscientific, but we will consider it anyway). Let us assume that the resurrection of an *ordinary* man is indeed incredible. But such a line of reasoning cannot apply to the One whom we are considering. He was unique: in all He did; in all He said, in all He was. Whatever way we look at Him, He is in a class by Himself. Even apart from the resurrection, there are excellent and convincing reasons for believing that He was "God manifest in the flesh." [276]

---

[275] The basis of Anderson's arguments focus on the authenticity of the interaction between Christ and various individuals, the absence of credible alternatives, the number of incidents and the dramatic change in the disciples from being a group of uncertain people to driven apostles, many of whom went to their deaths without reneging on what would have been a myth if it had been concocted or the result of a group delusion. The full text of his argument can be found at https://biblicalstudies.org.uk/article_resurrection_anderson.html Please note the current copyright holder is unknown.

[276] The Evidence for the Resurrection, page 27. The online version is not identical to this extract from the published version but the overall sense is the same.

It is as if Anderson is also baffled by the science and cannot see a way round it. Here are two stories about the idea of dying and coming back to life. This first account from Minnesota CBS in 2001 is about a small boy who was only two years old when he wandered out of his house at night into the cold and was found dead by his father in the morning.

On a winter night, most children are warm in their beds. But 10 years ago, a mother and father awoke to discover their 2-year-old was missing. He'd wandered out of their farmhouse near Eau Claire in the middle of the night.[277] By the time anyone realized the boy was missing, he was seemingly dead. His body temperature had dropped to 60 degrees. The human heart stops at 72…

They started with warm fluids and IVs. Then Paulie's blood was circulated through a heart-lung machine. 'You can explain parts of it through science,' said Robert Weichmann, the cardiac surgeon who was as surprised as anyone when Paulie's heart came back to life. 'There had to be a miraculous event to allow this to happen and be what it is today,' said Weichmann. 'There had to be some wonderful spirit inside this young boy.'

The 2-year old boy who survived a night in the cold is now a typical sixth-grader. Doctors worried that his internal organs or brain might be damaged because blood flow had stopped for nearly three hours. But today Paulie has got good grades and even plays on the football team. (Gilbertson)

---

[277]   Eau Claire is a city in the west-central part of the U.S. state of Wisconsin.

The cardiac surgeon certainly did not regard it as a commonplace event. Not surprisingly, the blogs that follow this story are a mixture of belief in divine intervention and denial of any such cause, but they should not detract from the fact that this actually happened.

The second story is about a frog. This account does not appear to draw the same degree of religious controversy as the first.

Meet the Wood Frog: The Wood frog, a small variety of frog found in North America is one such creature. You ask what's so interesting about them? It is probably one of the most freeze tolerant beings. In other words, extracellular freeze tolerance and intracellular freeze avoidance enables the frog to do what it does. … When it touches the first bits of winter snow, a signal sets off in its body and the signal starts the blood freezing process. All the water is pulled away from the core of its organs and the water gets frozen. Putting all the organs in a shell of solid ice. The whole frog becomes hard as a rock and sits there like that for weeks. Till it sees the spring time. The most amazing part is that, during this time, the frog doesn't breathe, its heart stops beating and even kidneys stop functioning. In medical terms it could be called dead. In reality, it is only temporarily dead … And then spring comes. It thaws itself out without any cellular injury and starts jumping again. It dies in winter and comes back to life in the next season. (Pant)[278]

What these two stories highlight for all is the *mystery* involved in scientific exploration rather than anything categorical about divine

---

[278] Anupum Pant's article , A : 'Wood frog dies and comes back to life', can be found at *http://awesci.com/wood-frog-dies-and-comes-back/*

intervention. Our understanding of the natural world *does* involve regularities, but like David Hume, we should take into account the principle that because A has always followed B, we cannot infer that A *will always* follow B. So when Anderson suggests that we cannot apply the "line of reasoning" to Christ that we can to an "ordinary man", he may be making the mistake of thinking there is potentially no scientific explanation of the resurrection.[279] Perhaps it is more realistic to assume that we are still in the foothills of learning about such unusual events. There are exceptions to the rule and those exceptions involve physical changes.[280] So for instance, Paulie says "The end of my fingers here, the nerves they ain't as strong as all the other ones … This one was worse; this one was underneath my chest" (Gilbertson). A complete suspension of natural processes would surely have left no marks at all.

What do these examples show? It seems that we can easily adopt a somewhat fixed view of science through the teaching of known scientific principles in our education system and through the many instructive documentaries on television. We can be so confident about what we already know that when we are faced with irregularities, we might be more prone to classify them as myth rather than opening doors to yet undiscovered knowledge. When others report a miracle, we can either agree, look for a way of explaining it or classify it as a product of the imagination. The idea that something can both be a miracle and have a yet unknown scientific explanation is not a response which is normally considered to be a realistic possibility. We are familiar with being entertained by

---

[279] *The Evidence for the Resurrection*, page 4

[280] I have noted earlier that physicists assert that there is a place where the general theory of relativity gives way to quantum mechanics. See "Scientific Laws – Are They Universal?" in Chapter 1.

magicians and illusionists, knowing there is a technique to the trick but being completely unaware of what it is, even though we know it is not a 'miracle'.

Appendix 2

Moral Awareness[281]

I have argued in the text for a balance between mind and heart, for a space to include faith into our understanding of life, and, even though it has not been the main thrust of the argument, for a set of moral principles which we can use when working out moral problems. The reason why I find Christ's summary of the law so appealing is it combines the worship of God and love for our neighbours as a combination of both mind and heart. The worship of God translates into understanding our own limited perspective on the 'ladder' of knowledge and the love of neighbour invites us to adopt a 'Good Samaritan' gaze on the world around us. My view is that guiding principles can be elicited from a higher source, but those principles must be worked out using our *own* cognitive capacities in dealing with each situation as it arises.

I want to briefly look at how the concept of morality fits in with, for want of a better term, the rest of life. Bernard Williams argues the division moral philosophy has created between itself and the rest of the world is a false and ultimately self-defeating one.

---

[281] This appendix uses an amended section of my Doctoral Thesis, which I completed in 1992.

The purity of morality, its insistence on abstracting the moral consciousness from other kinds of emotional reaction or social influence, conceals not only the means by which it deals with deviant members of its community, but also the virtues of those means.[282]

Williams argues that the idea of an unquestionable moral code unwittingly conveys the image of 'compliance' from an alien source; rather, he proposes that reflection should allow for realistic participation by everyone in ethical and social life. By using morality as a deterrent, its genuine qualities are concealed and, consequently, liable to be dismissed. In other words, if we see 'morality' as a big stick, we miss out on the proper consideration we have to give to the relative importance of our own needs compared to those of others, regardless of the terms we couch them in.

'Morality' can be seen as an outdated relic of Victorian times, no longer required for twenty first century life. These days people are sufficiently aware of political, economic and social issues to make their own decisions as to whose interests they consider most important. They do not have to surrender their minds to an automatic dogma called 'morality', the sole function of which is to issue instructions without giving reason. Williams describes the 'gap' in the following way: "Morality makes people think that without its very special obligation, there is only inclination; without its utter voluntariness, there is only force; without its ultimately pure justice, there is no justice."[283] He goes on to show that philosophy has unwittingly contributed to the demise of 'morality' by both bureaucratising it and, in contrast, elevating it out of reach. In William's words, "The resources of modern philosophy are

---

[282] *Ethics and the Limits of Philosophy*, page 195
[283] Ibid, page 196

not well adjusted to the modern world. I have tried to show that this is partly because it is too much and too unknowingly caught up in it, unreflectively appealing to administrative ideas of rationality. In other ways, notably its more Kantian forms, it is not involved enough; it is governed by a dream of a community of reason that is too far removed as Hegel first said it was, from social and historic reality and from any concrete sense of ethical life – farther removed from those things, in some ways, than the religion it replaced." [284]

Williams rejects what is, in his view, the artificial polarity between moral systems which prescribe rules for every man and woman and the fabric of social life where luck, moral indifference, practical considerations and social distance are as relevant as ethical thinking. He seeks to place ethical thought within this latter framework, wanting it to be *part* of life rather than a *prescription* for it. Peter Singer's book, *The Expanding Circle: Ethics and Socio-Biology,* falls into the same trap that Williams warns against. Singer maintains that his interpretation of 'reason' will debunk all others.

Singer – Genetics and Reason

Singer suggests that in human history ethics have emerged simultaneously with the development of reason. This emergence has come from a background of genetically-based impulses where social animals are "prompted by their genes to help and refrain from injuring selected other animals". Singer sees the transformation into full blown ethics like this:

Altruistic impulses (which are genetically based) once limited to one's kind and one's own group might be extended to a wider

---

[284] *Ethics and the Limits of Philosophy*, page 197-8

circle by reasoning creatures who can see that they and their kin are one group among others and from that impartial point of view are no more important than others.[285]

He then goes on to imply that the emergence of reason from genetically powered altruism is enough for us to elevate it to a pure, undefiled and honed form of reflection.

There is a rational component to ethics. Taking an objective point of view involves seeing our own interests as no more important than the like interests of anyone else. If this, and this alone, is the rational component of ethics, there should be a debunking explanation – biological or cultural – for every other aspect of our conventional ethical beliefs, from the trite moral rules against lying and stealing to such noble constructions as justice and human rights. If so, when the debunked principles have been scrutinised, found wanting and cleared away we will be left with nothing but the impartial rationality of the principle of equal consideration of interests.[286]

Singer's version of reason appears to relegate the significance of all other accounts of ethical life, including concepts like justice and human rights. He describes such ideas, along with religious and moral law, as influences which reason can debunk. Singer's elevation of reason implies he cannot accept that reason can be a tool for destructive purposes: for a country to bomb another territory because there is a perceived threat to national security is to employ reasoning to justify the overall mission. Furthermore, he does not

---

[285]   *The Expanding Circle: Ethics and Socio-Biology*, page 134
[286]   Ibid, pages 150-1

understand that reasons can describe feelings and that feelings can emerge from reasoning.

Alternatively, Professor Patricia Churchland says that our sense of morality is "rooted in nothing more than our mammalian origins." [287]She maintains, like Singer, that evolution is the springboard of morality. However, she is also clear that the neurobiological story cannot of itself solve the moral problems we face: "none of it bears directly on any specific moral question; none of it sets us on a direct path from neural function to the "right" moral norms." [288] This is a more balanced evolutionary account than Singer's. Nevertheless, as I have argued, the sole reliance on the theory of evolution to explain human experience is unsustainable even without the incorporation of transcendence. This is because relativity and quantum theory can also claim to be equally relevant to the flourishing of life.

Where Does Morality Fit In?

Hume grounded morality in terms of a social arrangement, while Kant sought to justify pure reason as the true source of moral inspiration. Hume's account of justice referred to the limitations of sympathetic impulse as being the reason why a public system of justice is needed. Being a necessary form of social manipulation, it contradicts any absolute belief in the substantive reality of 'moral goodness'. Human behaviour is aggregated into a standardized form of motivation so that a standardized form of administrative morality can be worked out. It is flexible in that it is not underpinned by any unchangeable belief; it is rigid in that it presupposes all human motivation originates from self-centred instincts. Kant's account, on the other hand, creates an enormous chasm between the pure

---

[287] *New Scientist,* Vol. 243, No. 3249, Sept 2019, page 47
[288] *New Scientist,* Vol. 243, No. 3249, Sept 2019, page 47

reason of an unstained rational agent and the, by comparison, feeble experiences of frail human beings. Its self-professed omnipotence seems too distant to affect the web of emotional, political, economic and moral feelings which impinge on people living in a complex society. Hume took what might be regarded as a pessimistic view of the extent of moral sympathy, while Kant took a highly optimistic position as to the human capacity for implementing the dictates of reason above all else, paradoxically suggesting that there may be no known examples of 'pure reason'.

When it comes to belief in a transcendent moral force, the key question is whether such a belief rules out the sense that morality has to be **made by us**: in other words, are we active participants in forming the morality we live by or are we simply 'soldiers' taking orders? The history of religious institutions, which lean towards rigid orthodoxy, is littered with examples of the latter. Considering other people's interests in relation to our own is indeed a core theme of moral activity, as opposed to it being something we either do or do not do. We can quite easily give some weight to a moral perspective when considering an economic issue or the use of a scientific discovery. This does not mean we have to replace all economic issues with moral ones.[289]

The following example illustrates my approach. Take the issue of having to turn off a life support machine for a terminally ill relative.[290] One could take into account two apparently conflicting principles: firstly, the injunction not to kill and secondly, the command to love one's neighbour as oneself. These are both in themselves self-evidently 'good'. We might think that should we be in the position of

---

[289] This integrative approach is what Bernard Williams is pointing towards.
[290] Turning off a life support machine is not a criminal offence, but I am using it as an example of an action which ends someone's life.

the sufferer, we would want the machine turned off, even though it would end our life; loving our neighbour despite the fact this could be interpreted as 'killing'. The point is that there is a dilemma between the two principles and we cannot claim to be obeying one of them without there being a potential implication for the other. Despite the injunctions deriving their force from the Bible, *we* must resolve the dilemma facing us – if we are mindful of the two principles, we will have to work out what to do in those circumstances. On this account it is perfectly possible to be an active participant in ***deciding*** what moral action to take at the same time as holding a belief in a divine source of morality. To simply obey orders appears to be a denial of human flourishing. It is far more preferable, in my view, to integrate a moral approach into the wider aspects of life – belief in a transcendent God does not absolve the believer from exercising their conscience on a daily basis.

Appendix 3

Some examples of the misapplication of the Christian faith. Extracts are summaries unless otherwise indicated with quotation marks – the source is referenced at the end of each box.

> In 380, Roman Emperor Theodosius made belief in Christianity a matter of imperial command, ordering the people to adopt the name of catholic Christians. Those who refused were categorised as insane and made themselves liable to judgement, firstly from God and secondly from the Empire itself. The Emperor assumed that He himself was qualified to act on behalf of God in deciding and enacting His judgement.
>
> Stevenson, J, Ed. *A New Eusebius*, 1957.
> Gascoigne, B, *Christianity*, Revised Edition, Robinson, 2003.

> Ten years later in 390, whilst Emperor Theodosius was still on the throne, a riot took place in Thessalonica after a popular figure was imprisoned. The Governor of Thessalonica was killed during the riot. The Emperor tricked five thousand of the local population into attending a performance and, once inside the arena, saw to it that the five thousand people were slaughtered. Bishop Ambrose refused to give the Emperor communion until he had publicly acknowledged his wrongdoing. Eventually the Emperor did ask for a pardon and received communion from Bishop Ambrose.
>
> Gascoigne, B, *Christianity*, Revised Edition, Robinson, 2003.

In 772, Saxons in North West Germany were in the custom of worshiping pagan Gods. An English missionary had been living in the area attempting to convert the locals. Charlemagne led an army into the area bearing the name of Christianity. Records indicate that on one day, 4,500 Saxons were put to death for not converting to Christianity by being baptised.

Gascoigne, B, *Christianity*, Revised Edition, Robinson, 2003.

In the seventh century, Syria was captured by the Syrians, but in a particular village the Christians there were allowed by the Muslim invaders to carry on practising their faith. This tolerance of other faiths is referred to in the Quran and was used to justify the freedom to exercise Christian faith in a Muslim country. However, the climate radically changed when the Crusaders reached Syria. St Bernard claimed that the death of a Muslim was an act which glorified Christ. When the First Crusade, after massacring very large numbers of Jews, in Germany reached Jerusalem, the bloodbath that followed was unimaginable; Jews who took refuge in the synagogue were burnt alive.

> With drawn swords our people ran through the city; nor did they spare anyone, not even those pleading for mercy … Not one of them was allowed to live. They did not spare the women or children. The horses waded in blood up to their knees, nay up to the bridle. It was a just and wonderful judgement of God.

Quote: Cohn, N, The Pursuit of the Millennium, Secker & Warburg, 1957.
Context: Gascoigne, B, *Christianity*, Revised Edition, Robinson, 2003.

"At the end of the twelfth century Innocent III became Pope and under him the Church of Western Europe reached the height of its power. He and his immediate successors are responsible for imagining and beginning an organized movement to sweep heretics out of Christendom ... the Pope announced a Crusade against the Albigeois, and offered to all who would bear a hand the usual rewards granted to Crusaders, including absolution from all their sins. A series of sanguinary wars followed in which the Englishman, Simon de Montfort, took part. There were wholesale burnings and hangings of men, women and children. The resistance of the people was broken down, though the heresy was not eradicated, and the struggle ended in 1229 with the complete humiliation of the Count of Toulouse. The important point of the episode is this: the Church introduced into the public law of Europe the new principle that a sovran held his crown on the condition that he should extirpate heresy. If he hesitated to persecute at the command of the Pope, he must be coerced; his lands were forfeited; and his dominions were thrown open to be seized by any one whom the Church could induce to attack him. The Popes thus established a theocratic system in which all other interests were to be subordinated to the grand duty of maintaining the purity of the Faith."

Bury J. B, A History of Freedom of Thought, Henry Holt and Company, University Press, Cambridge USA, 1913. http://www.criticalthinking.org/pages/a-history-of-freedom-of-thought/649 (Accessed 20 June 2018)

In 1532, in the city of Munster, the pastor and some prominent people converted to an extreme form of Baptist teaching. They became known as the Anabaptists. The city was placed under siege by the Bishop who had been expelled, and a man called Jan Bockeson became the Anabaptist leader. He was a polygamist and had sixteen wives. It is thought he beheaded one of them himself in public after a dispute with her.

Byrie, A, *Protestants*, William Collins, London, 2017.

"In 1553, a Spaniard named Miguel Servetus came to Geneva. "Radical" hardly does justice to Servetus, a brilliant physician and freethinker who denied the doctrine of the Trinity, the authority of the Bible, and virtually everything else that respectable Christians held dear. He was already on the run from the Inquisition. Virtually any territory in Europe would have executed him, and Calvin, who had read his books with horror, had warned him never to come to Geneva. When Servetus came nevertheless, he was arrested, tried for heresy, and, eventually burned alive."

Byrie, A, *Protestants*, William Collins, London, 2017, pg. 74.

"During the first religious war of 1562-63, virtually all French Christians became entrenched with one of the two religious parties, and thereafter viewed each other as enemies.

The violence ran both ways. Protestants took over several towns, sometimes slaughtering the Catholic leadership and often targeting Catholic priests and defiling Catholic churches. They mutilated the saints' statues, which they believed to be blasphemous idols. Female saints' statues were liable to have their noses cut off, as if they were syphilitic whores. But most popular violence was driven by the Catholic majority, urged by their preachers to purify communities polluted by heretics living in their midst. Paris became a cauldron of anti-Protestant hatred."

Byrie, A, *Protestants*, William Collins, London, 2017, pg. 92-3.

"Emotional excess became a feature of American religious life during the eighteenth century. It was especially evident in the First Great Awakening which erupted in Northampton, Connecticut, in 1734 ... Within six months three hundred people in the town had experienced a wrenching 'born-again' conversion. They alternated between soaring highs and devastating lows ... When the revival died down in Northampton, one man was so cast down he committed suicide, convinced that the loss of ecstatic joy could only mean he was predestined to Hell."

Armstrong, K, *The Battle for God*, Harper Perennial, London, 2000 pg. 78-9.

The white-dominated 'Dutch Reformed Church' supported apartheid, arguing from the Bible that God deliberately divided people into different races (see Genesis 11 – This account ... gives no indication that one language group should dominate another but was used to suggest that the whites were superior to blacks). The Bible says: There is no longer Jew or Gentile, slave or free, male or female. For you are all Christians –you are one in Christ Jesus (Galatians 3:28).

http://request.org.uk/issues/social-issues/case-study-apartheid/ (Accessed 7 June 2018)

"The German Christians tried, vainly, to demonstrate the compatibility of their beliefs with Nazism. In 1939, eleven regional churches produced a declaration describing Christianity 'as the irreconcilable religious opposite of Judaism' ... During the war, some German Christian churches took to declaring themselves 'officially anti-Jewish.'"

Byrie, A, *Protestants*, William Collins, London, 2017, pg. 276.

"The evangelical culture ties together faithfulness with extroversion ... The emphasis is on community, on participating in more and more programs and events, on meeting more and more people. It's a constant tension for many introverts that they're not living that out. And in a religious world, there's more at stake when you feel that tension. It doesn't feel like 'I'm not doing as well as I'd like.' It feels like 'God isn't pleased with me.' "

Cain, S, *Quiet, The Power of Introverts in a World That Can't Stop Talking*, Penguin, New York, 2012, pg. 66.

Index

50 Great Myths about Atheism
(Blackford and Schuklenk)
129, 130, 164
abortion 164
abuse
and rationality 82
religious 10, 55, 133–5, 149,
164–5, 195
adaptation
environmental 115, 120–1
evolutionary 75
'Adversarial Collaboration' 152n200
agnosticism 50–1, 56, 64
Al-Kahlili, Jim 176
Albigeois 233
Alexander, Dennis 52n51, 89
altruism 53, 188, 225–6
Ambrose, Bishop 231
Anabaptists 234
Anderson, JND, The Evidence For
The Resurrection 217, 218,
220
anger 28–30, 86n91
Anne Frank - In the Secret Annexe
146
Apartheid 80
Areo magazine 134
Aristotle 37-38
Armstrong, Karen 157, 195
The Battle for God 178–80, 182,
183

artificial intelligence 43
artificial selection 9, 11, 107, 115,
161, 190, 193
aspiration 55, 82, 109, 187, 198
atheism 15, 51, 56–8, 129, 134, 135,
136, 148, 151, 159, 162, 164, 171
and faith 15
and hell 146
and hypocrisy 165
and transcendence 11,
123n150, 193
authority 137, 140, 148n195, 151,
157, 192, 194, 198
autonomy 42–3, 53, 160
Ayrton, Hertha 140

Barker, Wesley 76–9, 80
behaviour
animal 59
human 52, 117, 120, 153, 165,
188–9, 227
and truth 138–40
see also cooperation; morality;
relationships
belief 15, 30, 71n74, 119, 124, 126,
128–9, 134–5, 145–6, 148,
156, 193–4, 229
and behaviour 138–40, 164–5
and creation 91
and evolution 54, 100, 101, 107,
109, 110

and reason 86, 151
and science 180
Bennett, Jonathan 69
Bergson, Henri 122
Bernard, St 232
Bible, Gospels 51, 133
Bible, cited
      Genesis 65, 236
      St Mark's Gospel 144n191, 168,
            216
      St Luke's Gospel 165
      St John's Gospel 216
      Acts 2, 167
      1 Corinthians 100, 215, 216
      Galations 236
Big Bang theory 32, 33, 91n95, 102
black holes 91n95, 116, 173, 181, 199
Blackford, Russell and Schuklenk, 50
      Great Myths about Atheism
            129, 130, 164
The Blind Watchmaker *(Dawkins)*
            90, 190
Bockeson, Jan 234
Broadie, Alexander 56, 57
Broome, John 73, 74, 75, 79, 82,
            86n91, 155, 158
      Rationality Through Reasoning
            96
Bruce, Frederick Fyvie 131, 132, 217
      The New Testament Documents
            - Are They Reliable
            216n274
Bryant, Levi 111
Buddhism 141
Burger, Dr Jerry 136
Burundi 150

Cambodia 136, 150

capital punishment 164
carbon dating 54
Cartwright, Jon 194
Categorical Imperative 81–2
chance, and design 50, 58–9, 104, 176
chaos 104, 123, 124, 127
charisma 151, 157
Charlemagne 232
China 136, 144
Christ see Jesus Christ
Christianity 131, 132, 141, 143n189,
            144n191, 179
      misapplication 231–6
Christie, Sandy 166–7
Churchland, Patricia 120, 121, 122,
            227
climate change 115, 193
Clutton-Brock, Tim 119–20
cognition 9, 10, 35, 38, 43, 49, 50, 87,
            88, 115–16, 156–7
      and emotion 40, 42, 159, 160,
            180
      see also mind
cognitive capacity 41, 42, 62, 87, 89,
            149, 223
commerce 156
communication 39, 40, 163, 180–1
Communism 134, 136
conflict 16, 100, 117, 150, 188
      and religion 143–5
conscience 164, 229
consciousness 24n11, 41, 80, 97, 119,
            120, 125–7, 177, 224
consumption 191, 193
cooperation 22, 39, 55, 88, 119–20,
            164, 189, 191, 193
cosmology 97
courage 108, 148, 149, 153

creation 49, 127
  and evolution 58–62, 67, 87,
    88–9, 162
  see also intelligent design
The Creation Science Journal 92
creationist theology, and rationality
  67, 85–97, 162
Creator God 7, 11, 15, 51, 56–8, 60,
  64, 102, 177
  and evolutionists 58–62
crucifixion 168
Crusades 134, 232, 233
culture 15, 41, 43, 47, 52, 87,
  156n212, 171

Darwin, Charles 49, 50, 51, 52, 95,
  97, 109, 110
  Origin of Species 34, 54, 99
Dawkins, Richard 95, 164
  Outgrowing God 131n163
  The Blind Watchmaker 90, 190
  The God Delusion 55, 95, 97,
    133
  The Greatest Show on Earth
    54, 61, 110n117, 114,
    121n143
De Bellaigue, Christopher 141–2
de Montford, Simon 233
death 38, 100, 146, 178
decision making 16, 43, 44, 47, 88,
  108, 127, 154n203
Deleuze, Gilles 122, 122–5
delusion 63, 151, 155
Democratic Republic of Congo 150
democratic society 80, 110, 158, 191
Dennett, Daniel 39, 43, 46, 90, 93, 96
Descartes, René 38, 39
design

and chance 50, 58–9, 104, 176
  see also intelligent design
determinism 53, 61, 62
Dialogues (Hume) 56
diet 184n252
divination 151, 157
DNA 15, 27, 63n65, 95, 101, 104,
  110n117, 118, 161
dogma 80, 151, 157, 190, 224
Domasio, Antonio 46, 63, 121–2, 159,
  160
  Looking for Spinoza 42
  The Strange Order of Things 47,
    106, 121
du Sautoy, Marcus 33, 34, 103n113,
  162
du Toit, Cornel 53
Dutch Reformed Church 80, 236

Eagleman, David 41, 42, 43
Edwards, Tim 5, 60, 62, 91n95,
  137n177, 167, 182n251,
  184n252, 185, 190, 191, 192,
  201
Einstein, Albert, General Law of
  Relativity 32
emotions 29, 31, 34, 35, 40, 41–2, 44,
  47, 95, 97, 118, 129, 133, 159,
  160
empathy 29
empiricism 142, 181, 182
enkrasia 74, 86n91
  see also rationality
Enlightenment 15, 56, 79, 94, 149,
  151–69
entropy, and perception of time 154,
  171, 172–8
environment 14, 33n21, 64, 72, 104,

110, 114, 115, 120–1, 140, 174,
        184, 191
ethics 52, 77, 110, 117, 190, 225–6
Euclid 25
evangelical culture 236
evolution 9, 10, 13, 16, 40, 41, 42, 44,
        46, 90, 106, 124, 161–3, 175–6
    and creation 58–62, 67, 87,
        88–9, 162
    and genetic mutation 7, 33
    and God 11, 15, 51–2, 54,
        58–62, 162, 168
    and human nature 188–9
    and human relations 52–6
    and immanence 109–28
    and intelligent design 49, 65
    as metatheory 99–108
    and morality 164, 227
    and rationality 85–97
    and time 102–3, 114, 116, 174
existentialism 23
experience 26–30, 38, 42, 47, 57, 60,
        72, 79, 82, 83, 95, 96, 112–13,
        118–19, 123, 152, 155, 158,
        167, 202, 227

faith 11, 13, 15–16, 53, 60n60, 78–9,
        157, 166–7, 183–4, 202
    misapplication 76–9, 231–4
    and oppression 129–50
    and reason 8, 151, 152, 161–3
    and science 171–84
Father Christmas 55
fear 57, 145, 151, 158
feelings 10, 25–7, 28–30, 34–5, 40, 42,
        95, 121, 129, 151, 153, 157–8,
        188
    and reason 7, 15, 158–60, 163,

        168–9, 227
First Cause argument 50, 101–3, 107
First Great Awakening 235
Fordyce, John 51
Foucault, Michel 140n179
foundationalism 26n.14
free choice 47, 197
French Revolution 34
French Wars of Religion 235

Galileo 153
gender reassignment 115
genetic inheritance 43, 104, 188
genetic manipulation 62–3, 161, 162,
        191–2
genetic mutation 22, 27, 33, 110n117,
        115, 174
genetics 15, 47, 91, 100, 162
    and reason 225–6
genocide 137
Gettier, Edmund 20, 21
Gilbertson 218, 220
God
    character 57, 105, 159
    and evolution 11, 15, 51–2, 54,
        58–62, 162, 164
    existence 11, 50, 51, 64, 109,
        117, 133, 159, 160, 201
    incarnate see Jesus Christ
    relationship with 100, 147, 166
Godfrey-Smith, Peter 189
Goodwin, Thomas 166
Grayling, A.C. 38n27
Great Internet Mersenne Prime Search
        25
Greek philosophy 37
Greene, Joshua 188–90
Gregg, Heather Selma 141, 144

grief 59
'Groundhog Day' (film) 34
Guantanomo Bay 137n177
Guattari, Félix 124

Harari, Yuval Noah 156, 161, 192
Haught, JF. 164
Hawking, Stephen 32, 90, 102,
    159n217
    Brief Answers to the Big
        Questions 173, 175, 181,
        191, 192
Hegel, Georg Wilhelm Friedrich 123,
    225
hell 50, 145-8
heresy 233, 234
hermeneutics 151
higher moral authority 194, 198
Hinduism 141
Hitchens, Christopher 137, 148n195
    god is not Great 133, 134
Hodge, Charles 179n242
Homo Sapiens 7, 53, 156, 161
Horowitz, MC 144
Hubble's law 34
human nature 10, 57, 65, 104, 138,
    140, 148-9, 187-200
Hume, David 28, 30, 31, 40n33, 56, 61,
    82, 104, 111, 160, 220, 227, 228
    Dialogues 56
Huntington's disease 22

identity 30-2, 110, 123
imagination 42, 45, 64, 71n74, 91,
    102, 105, 155-8, 181, 183, 220
immanence 41, 49, 109-28, 190
impulse 156, 225, 227
induction principle 29, 32, 33

Innocent III, Pope 233
Inquisition 134, 234
intelligent design 47, 49-60, 61-2,
    64, 65, 90, 104-6, 107, 161,
    176-7, 201
intelligent redesign 49-66, 161-3
intentionality 15, 31, 58-60, 85-97, 103,
    117, 163
    and randomness 58-62, 103
    internal coherence 10, 65n69, 73-6,
        78, 82, 85, 96
    intuitions 95, 129, 190
Iraq 150
Islam 141-2, 143, 144n191, 147n194,
    179, 232
Israel Antiquities Authority 132
IVF treatment for infertility 115

Japan 144
Jarvie, Ian 72, 77, 81
Jesus Christ 11, 15, 60n60, 129, 132,
    144n191, 148, 160, 168, 199,
    200, 202
    commandments 160, 168-169, 223
    God incarnate 15, 60n60, 160,
        164, 216
    on hell 146-7
    historicity 129-33
    moral indignation 147, 163,
        164-6
    resurrection 215-21
Jews see Judaism
Jones, Steve 99-101
    In the Blood - God, Genes and
        Destiny 100
Josephus, Flavius 130-1
Judaism 141, 143n189, 144n191, 179,
    230, 232

judgement 145-8, 231, 232
Jung, Carl 46, 125
justice 68, 164, 165, 224, 226, 227
justification 20n3, 23-5, 26, 30, 80

Kac, Eduardo 161, 163
Kalanithi, Paul, When Breath
     becomes Air 180n245
Kang, DC 144
Kant, Immanuel
     and evolution 126
     and immanence 122
     and materialism 115-18
     and rationality 79-81, 195, 196,
          197, 225
     and reason 111-15, 227-8
Kemp-Smith, Norman 114
Kepler, Johannes 24
Khmer Rouge 136
kin loyalty 53
kindliness 108, 148, 149
Knapton, Sarah 22
knowledge 9, 16, 19-33, 37, 44, 60-63,
     82-83, 94-97, 105, 108-111,
     116-117, 122, 127
     see also scientific knowledge;
          self-knowledge
Korea 144

language 26, 35, 40, 69, 93, 121, 124-
     125, 182
Laplace, Pierre-Simon 153
laughing 57
Lazarus 216
Levin, Margarita Rosa 21, 22
logos, and mythos 178-83
love, and judgement 145-8
lying 75, 196, 226

McFadden, Jonjoe 176
Macintyre, Alasdair 68, 72, 74
Maier, Paul 130, 131
Maoist China 136
Marcus Aurelius 77, 81
materialism 49, 68, 90, 115-18, 126, 216
mathematics 9, 159
matter, from nothing 90-2
Mayr, Ernst 51, 52, 53
memes 43, 46, 88
memory 42, 44, 45, 46, 192
Middle East 150
Milgram, Stanley 136-7
mind-body debate 9, 15, 35, 37-47,
     154n203
Minnesota CBS 218
morality 117, 119, 120, 163-5, 169,
     187, 194n264, 195, 223-9
Muluk, H 143
Munster 234
Muslims see Islam
mysticism 151, 157
myth 156, 168, 171, 178-83
Mythos 195
     and logos 178-83

natural clocks 54
natural law argument 103-4
natural selection 33, 40, 51, 58, 61,
     63, 97, 99, 100-1, 106-7, 110,
     161, 191, 192
natural world 15, 22, 46, 49, 64-65,
     81, 104, 105, 110, 111, 159,
     160, 171, 174, 176, 182, 183,
     188, 198, 220
     redesign 7, 16, 63-64, 161-3, 201
Nazism 236
neurology 15, 37, 42-6, 154n203, 160

neutral mutations 114
New Enlightenment Project 151–169
Newton, Isaac 153
Northampton, Connecticut 235
Northern Ireland 145
Nozik, Robert 21n.5

objectivity 21, 94, 171
oppression, and faith 129–50, 54, 99
Origin of Species (Darwin) 34, 50, 54, 99
Ostenfield, Erik 38
out of body experiences 60

Paisner, Matthew 20
Pant, Anupum 219
passions 15, 28–30, 64, 82, 160
Penrose, Roger 91
philosophy 5, 13–15, 37, 41, 121, 135, 152, 223–4
Piaget, Jean 112n119
Pinker, Stephen 128, 140n180, 151–5, 158
The Blank State 188–9
Planck, Max 90, 172, 175
Plato 37, 38
Pol Pot 136
positivism 41, 51
poverty 82, 154
prediction 29, 40n33, 44–5, 72, 76, 81–2, 82, 104, 115, 122, 177, 191
prejudging the unknowns 92, 94–5
Proust, Joelle 39, 40

qualitative values (purpose) 184n252
quantum physics 10, 194, 198, 199
quantum theory 10, 32, 107, 115, 116, 172, 176, 190

Quine, Willard Van Ormon 112n120
Quran 143, 197n272, 232

rabbit, fluorescent green (Alba) 161, 163
rain dances 72
randomness
and intentional creativity 58–62, 62–4, 99
and natural selection 7, 44, 88, 103–4, 107, 110, 114–15, 116, 174
rationality 9–10, 16, 31, 65, 67–83, 122, 127, 150, 182, 195–6
and evolution 85–97
and intentionality 72, 73, 85–97
see also reason
reason 10, 13, 14, 15, 16, 38, 42, 44, 65n69, 67, 69, 75, 82, 86, 110, 111–15, 118, 128, 135
and faith 151, 152, 161–3
and feelings 15, 50, 158–60, 168
and genetics 225–6
see also rationality
reciprocity, and cooperation 119–20
relationships 9, 13, 27, 35, 52–6, 106, 155–8, 158, 184n252
relativity 32, 90, 107, 176, 227
religion 14–16, 46, 118–22, 125, 155–8, 187
and abuse 55, 133–7, 138, 139, 148, 164, 183
and conflict 143–5
and evolution 10, 15
and hypocrisy 164–5
and imagination 155–8
and moral indignation 163–5
and myth 178–83
and science 49, 53, 101, 109–

10, 183–4
and violence 140–5
religious tolerance 195–9
respect 81–2, 117, 182, 195–7
resurrection 129, 133, 168, 215–21
child in Canada 168
revelation 110, 151, 157
ritual 178
Rölli, Marc 122
Romey, Kristen 132–3
Rosling, Hans 154
Rovelli, Carlo
Reality is Not what is Seems
180–1
Seven Brief Lessons in Physics
116
The Order of Time 113n123,
172, 173, 175–6
Russell, Bertrand 29n18, 101–6, 129,
132, 145–6, 148–50
Ruth, DM 143
Rwanda 150

San, Dr Abigail 136
Sartre, Jean-Paul 157
Saxons, in North West Germany 232
Schuklenk, Udo see *Blackford*
science 7, 10–11, 14, 21, 22, 23, 28, 32–
4, 35, 63–4, 96, 104, 135, 140
empirical 113
and faith 79, 101, 171–84
induction principle 29, 32, 33
and intentionality 31
and myth 178–83
and rationality 72, 76, 81
and reason 14, 16
and religion 14, 49, 51, 53, 101,
109, 177, 183–4, 187,

195, 198
scientific knowledge 7, 17, 22–4, 41,
57, 60, 89, 95, 103, 105–6, 124,
160, 163, 171, 172–8
application 63, 83
misuse 140, 149, 187
self
theory of 30–1
see also identity
self-awareness 23, 123
self-contradiction 72, 88
self-control 7, 191, 192
self-destruction 53, 67
self-discovery 149
self-interest 149, 227
self-knowledge 25–8, 37, 97
self-preservation 149, 188
Sellars, Wilfrid 25
Servetus, Miguel 234
sexuality 164
Shakespeare, William 45–6, 59
Simpson, OJ 27n15
Singer, Peter 225
*The Expanding Circle: Ethics
and Socio-Biology* 225
social cohesion 55
social control 195
social cooperation 10, 22, 164, 183,
199
social interaction 11, 120, 180–1, 189
social justice 14, 55, 56
social manipulation 227
social policy 10
social status 29
social stratification 156
society 10, 22, 52, 55, 68, 70, 125, 176
'Sophie's Choice' (film) 148
South Africa 150

Soviet Union 136
space and time 60, 61, 101–2, 113, 172
  origins 108
species advantage and development
  54, 56, 115, 126
Spencer, Herbert 50, 52, 54, 176
Spinoza, Baruch 38, 39, 61, 63
spirituality 35, 41, 49, 51, 97, 108,
  111, 117–19, 125, 133, 147,
  159, 167–8, 179–80, 184, 190,
  202
Stalin, Joseph 134
Stanford Encyclopaedia of
  Philosophy 123–4
Stanovitch, Keith, Who is Rational?
  75n81
Sterenly, Kim 87, 88
suffering 11, 134, 143, 168, 202
Sumaktoyo, NG 143
supernatural 53, 156
Svensson, I 143
Syria 232

Tabrizi, Sarah 22, 23
Tallis, Raymond 41, 42, 43
Talmudic debate 152
teleology 52, 117, 125, 126
  see also intelligent design
terror 57, 106
Thalidomide 76, 77
theatre 29
Theodosius, Emperor 231
theology, false assertions 163
Thorne, Kip 173, 181
time 33, 34, 101–3, 108, 113, 172
  and entropy 154, 171, 172–8
  and evolution 102–3, 114, 116, 174
  see also space
torture 135, 187
Toulouse, Count of 233

transcendence 41, 46, 49, 60, 90, 109,
  118, 123, 168, 193–5, 201
tree of cousinship 113, 121n143
tree rings 54
truth 19–21, 22, 27, 30, 138–40

unconscious 46, 65, 80, 125
universe, origins 108

Vallejo-Marin, Dr 63
Velman, Max 24n.11
Verhoef, Anné 53, 54, 109, 118–22,
  124, 125–6
Vietnam 144, 150
violence, and religion 80, 140–5, 235
visions 157
Voltaire 105

Weichmann, Robert 218
Weiss, Ittay 25
Whiston, William 130
Wicks, Robert 117, 195
  Kant, A Complete Introduction
  113
Williams, Bernard 223–5
Winch, Peter 14
Wittgenstein, Ludwig 26n13, 182
wood frog 219

xenophobia 55

Yemen 150
Yugoslavia (former) 150

Zel'dovich, Yakov Borisovich 181
Zimbardo, Philip 140n179
Zoroastrianism 152n199